YO
I

GEMINI

May 22 to June 21

ROGER ELLIOT

For June, a
June baby

Roger Elliot

Futura

A Futura Book

Copyright © Roger Elliot 1986

First published in Great Britain in 1986
by Futura Publications, a Division of
Macdonald & Co (Publishers) Ltd
London & Sydney

ISBN 0 7088 2894 9

Photoset in North Wales by
Derek Doyle & Associates, Mold, Clwyd.
Printed and bound in Great Britain by
Hazell, Watson & Viney Ltd,
Aylesbury, Bucks.

Futura Publications
A Division of
Macdonald & Co (Publishers) Ltd
Greater London House
Hampstead Road
London NW1 7QX

A BPCC plc Company

Contents

ROGER ELLIOT is one of the foremost astrologers in the world today. As a writer, TV performer, teacher and consultant to many individuals, he spans the full range of astrology from scientific research to newspaper columns.

Roger, born under Cancer, lives in a Somerset manor house with his blonde Australian wife Suzie, and two teenage children, Stephanie and Mark.

My World

of Astrology

Welcome to 1987. It's going to be an exciting year for many people, not least Gemini, and I'm delighted that once again I can guide you through the year ahead.

For six years I have produced this series of predictions for the different Zodiac signs, but this year is truly special. We have a new publisher, suitably called Futura, who are keen to expand the scope of these books. So these 1987 books are one-and-a-half times larger than the previous editions, which means I've been able to give much more detailed information on how the planets are influencing us all in the next twelve months. I hope you like these improvements.

The daily forecasts are now composed of two sections. The first half, *written in italic*, refers to the whole world and everyone in it. They give you an idea how other people are likely to behave on the day in question – indeed, they may give a clue to the national and international events taking place that day.

The second half of each daily forecast refers, as usual, to yourself – as a birth-child of Gemini – and the moods, events and circumstances that may occur in your individual life. Sometimes they match the generalised forecast, and sometimes they differ, simply because the planets that day are making a special pattern as far as your Zodiac sign is concerned.

Another addition in 1987 is the Wise Words at the end of each monthly prediction. These are quotations I have collected over the years which I found apt, true or witty, and I have chosen the appropriate saying for your life during the month in question. Perhaps my choice of quotations tells you more about myself than you! But I do feel that this quotation for each month can help to focus your thoughts – to inspire or amuse you, or give a word of warning, or touch your conscience.

Another improvement is the section Mixing With Others, which tells you more about other Zodiac signs besides your own. Let's hope you will now have a clearer idea about the way you relate to various birth-signs – as a friend or relative, employee, lover or spouse.

For newcomers to this horoscope series, let me repeat my approach to astrology. I do not believe our future is preordained – by God or the planets – but a course is plotted, and it's our task in life to follow this path, through good times and bad, *making the best possible journey we can*.

We may not be able to control all our circumstances, but we can respond to them with courage, humour, skill and love for others. To that extent, we are masters of our fate.

My task, in this Gemini account of your life in 1987, is to help you anticipate the future. For some reason that I cannot fathom, the pattern of human life seems to be reflected in the pattern of the sky above, which is constantly changing with some planets racing ahead, others plodding behind, and some of them darting back and forth.

To understand this pattern, I use computers to analyse the celestial movements and store an ever-increasing amount of information from you – the readers of this book. It does help greatly if you can write telling me which forecasts are true, using the address on page 95. In this way I am constantly updating my information, so that future books can be even more detailed and, hopefully, correct.

So do stay in touch. I like to think of all my readers, from Aberdeen to Zimbabwe, as part of a world-wide family of like-minded people. Some of us are sure that astrology works. Others may be more sceptical – at first, anyway! Hopefully you will gradually become convinced, as the months pass, that my kind of guidance is helpful, interesting and, in times of trouble, supportive. I do trust so.

Obviously, in a book of this size, referring to so many kinds of people – mothers, businessmen, school kids, pensioners and so forth – there will be remarks that may not directly apply to you. Well, be patient – and, if necessary, use your imagination to change the precise meaning into one that could refer to your individual circumstances.

And do remember that I'm always willing to help with personal problems. If you want to learn more about astrology, and get your own horoscope in some way, turn to page 94 for further details. Wherever you live, whatever your difficulties, your letter will reach me.

I am very conscious, as I write these words, that many of you, reading them, will be unhappy or anxious or unfulfilled. I cannot solve your life's problems – indeed, perhaps no one can. Certainly I cannot promise riches or romantic happiness or perfect health. But I can surround you in spiritual love, like an armour of silver light. So many people, uncertain what the future holds, get lonely or depressed. If so, please picture for yourself, as I am doing now, this shining silver aura holding you secure and safe.

It can heal you. It can make you hopeful again. It can help you to love the human race, however badly others have treated you in the recent past.

This is the aura of the Moon, the 'mother' who is constantly circling the Earth. She can bring peace into your heart. She can make you whole again.

We are all children of the stars. Nothing is really new. Every atom of our bodies was formed billions of years ago, in another part of the universe, and floated through space until it became part of our own solar system.

We came from the sky. We shall return there. We are part of the whole universe – and here, for our season on Earth, we are one family, a part of each other.

This may sound sentimental to some of you – but many others, I am sure, will know that it is true.

So let the great armour of light protect you. And let your energies blaze out in 1987.

ROGER ELLIOT

Technical

Note

Many people ask how I arrive at my predictions. My method is more scientific than other astrologers', but there may still be some psychic quality involved.

First of all, using my computers, I prepare an *ephemeris* for 1987 listing the positions of the Sun, Moon and planets for each day of the year. They are all grouped along a great circle in the sky called the *ecliptic* or *Zodiac*, which is divided into the twelve signs.

Then I prepare a daily *aspectarian* telling me which planets are in line with each other, or in opposition, or square to each other, or whatever it may be. Let's take Christmas Day as an example. On December 25 the Sun will be in line with Mercury, while Uranus will be mid-way between Venus and Mars. These are only two of 16 aspects in force that day.

Now each planet represents a different quality of life. So Mercury represents talking and sociability, while the Sun is our driving-force and willpower. So to have them both in a straight line means that Christmas Day will be a lively and friendly time for the whole world. At the same time, the place of Uranus mid-way between Venus and Mars means a lively sexual time for many people, with sudden friendships developing over a couple of drinks at a party.

That's why my general prediction for this festive day on page 93 is *Still a friendly day. Better to move around and mix*.

The individual forecast that follows is based on a careful analysis of what these planets mean for Gemini. Sometimes I am very scientific, noting the rulerships of the planets as far as you are concerned, and sometimes I simply get a mental picture of the various conflicting forces and imagine how a versatile, talented person like Gemini would respond!

Mixing

with others

You may think that just because you're a Gemini you have got nothing in common with Libra or Aquarius.

But in fact these three signs have a lot in common, because all the Zodiac signs are linked by an enthralling system of Elements and Modes. By discovering which Mode and Element you belong to, you can find out what you have in common with other signs – and what you don't!

The Modes

Aries, Cancer, Libra and Capricorn belong to the **Cardinal Mode.** All the Cardinal signs are concerned with activity. In their differing ways they like to get things moving; to take practical steps; to start a new enterprise. So they resemble the cardinal points of the compass – north, south, east and west – in the sense that they point in a new direction.

Taurus, Leo, Scorpio and Aquarius belong to the **Fixed Mode.** Fixed signs are exactly what they say they are: immovable and fixed, gaining strength from maintaining a situation rather than changing it. They have the virtue of persistence and the drawback of stubbornness.

If the Cardinal signs can be symbolised by a pointing finger, Fixed signs are represented by a clenched fist.

Gemini, Virgo, Sagittarius and Pisces belong to the **Mutable Mode**. Mutable signs express changeability. They are also called dualistic signs because their energy seems to fluctuate.

If Cardinal signs drive straight down the road, Mutable ones veer from side to side. This provides great flexibility of outlook, but also great unreliability and lack of constancy.

The Elements

Capricorn, Taurus and Virgo belong to the **Earth Element.** Earth signs are solid, reliable and stable. The world tends to approve of earthy people, although they can be rather crude and indelicate at times. We like their commonsense.

The drawback of these signs is their lack of enterprise and vision. They can become encased in materialism, and gradually action can become clogged by inertia.

Aries, Leo and Sagittarius belong to the **Fire Element.** All the Fire signs have a magical quality, enabling them to fire other people into activity. At their most creative, these signs have constant access to real enthusiasm. They are powered by an unending fuel store helping them to achieve a great deal. At their most destructive, however, the Fire signs use other people as fuel. They burn the energy out of them, leaving behind a trail of wrecked hearts.

Libra, Aquarius and Gemini belong to the **Air Element.** Air is an insubstantial Element. It breezes this way and that, carrying seeds from one part of the land to another. Traditionally it's linked with the transmission of ideas.

Air signs are communicative and sociable – bringing men and women together; spreading ideas and trying to change their surroundings. You can see the possible faults of these signs in the popular sayings 'too airy-fairy' or 'talking a lot of hot air'.

Cancer, Scorpio and Pisces belong to the **Water Element.** Water is the most mysterious of the four Elements. We are said to be born in the waters of the womb, or have evolved from earlier aquatic creatures, and spiritually we return to the great waters of eternity.

Water signs have a fine capacity to flow into the hearts and minds of other people. Like electricity through water, they are conducive to the ideas and feelings coming their way, and they respond very sensitively to their environment.

At worst, of course, they are wet, drippy and sloppy!

Aries

March 21 to April 20

Friendships Aries people like friends but hate to be dependent on them. They are self-reliant folk who, in the last resort, are quite happy on their own. They take friends at face value, and don't like people who are too moody or changeable or hanging back from making decisions. They enjoy the company of people who are enthusiastic, good-humoured and brave – just like themselves, in fact!

Sex Aries people are sexy, but that doesn't make them all Don Juans or nymphomaniacs. They have a strong, muscular sex nature that likes to impose itself on others. If anything, their sexuality is stronger than their need for love. Certainly they are self-centred people, and can ignore their partners' feelings.

Marriage Aries folk are not settlers by nature, but more like nomads or hunters. There's more fun for them in making new conquests than sticking with the same old mate. On the other hand, they hate failure – and what they have, they hold. So they can make loyal, stable marriage partners. If the marriage does get stale, Aries is the one to put a stop to the agony.

Aries (March 21 to April 20) and You

Both of you are busy, restless people, easily getting bored. But neither is resentful, and can be stimulating company.

An **Aries friend** isn't as subtle as you – more the outdoor type. But you make a lively pairing, full of projects and adventures. 1987 rating: very good this year.

With an **Aries parent** you have a strong-minded type who has pushed you around in the past. You both approach life in a positive spirit. 1987 rating: very warm and honest.

If you have an **Aries child** you have a practical type who is more direct than yourself. Plenty of rows, but able to look after himself. 1987 rating: first-rate.

An **Aries boy-friend** is a real hunk of man, but isn't as delicate a lover as you'd like. Plenty of arguments, which you each think you win! 1987 rating: eight out of ten.

An **Aries girl-friend** turns you on in a frank, no-nonsense way. You love talking about sex – she loves doing it! She's a cheerful girl. 1987 rating: time to kiss goodbye?

An **Aries husband** is independent, and goes his own way at weekends. He's not the type to sit and talk, as you love to. 1987 rating: will he be true?

An **Aries wife** will drive you hard – in your job and leisure activities. Lots of arguments, but all good, clean fun. You make an attractive, sociable couple. 1987 rating: easy-going.

Your **Aries boss** likes to throw his weight about. You can relieve the tension with laughter. 1987 rating: average to good. You may overtake him in some way.

Taurus

April 21 to May 21

Friendship Taurean people are among the most gregarious folk in the Zodiac. They love being surrounded by friends, and seek to form firm, solid friendships that last forever. It's part of the deep Taurean need for security. But there's a generous side to the bargain as well. They love plying their friends with food and drink, making them feel at home.

Sex Taurus is one of the sexiest of Zodiac signs. There is a basic earthiness about their approach to sex. They love living in their own bodies and, through kissing and touching, making contact with a loved one's body. They are highly sensual, and the danger is they'll make sex the be-all and end-all of their relationships. If the body loses appeal, they lose interest. A Taurean can too often

12

take the partner's feelings for granted.

Marriage Taureans are made for marriage. It's the most natural way for them to live, sharing with another and building up a strong, mutually supportive family. Ideally they are monogamist by nature, and want to stay faithful. They feel secure within marriage, and would only stray for sexual gratification. Otherwise they make loyal spouses.

Taurus (April 21 to May 21) and You

You can provide illuminating insights into each other's character. You seek variety, while Taurus prefers routine.

A **Taurus friend** is a careful type, a bit set in his ways. He will try to tie you down to a routine, which you won't like. 1987 rating: loving, but circumstances keep you apart.

A **Taurus parent** is a tower of strength in a crisis. At an everyday level, you don't always see eye to eye. But someone reassuring to come home to. 1987 rating: good advice needed.

A **Taurus child** gives little trouble. On the contrary, he or she is helpful, considerate if sometimes a little selfish. 1987 rating: good exam results, progress at college or work.

A **Taurus boy-friend** is amorous, and will make you feel like a woman. In the end he's a bit selfish, wanting you to put yourself out for him. 1987 rating: a temporary split-up?

A **Taurus girl-friend** is receptive to wooing – and once she's decided she likes you, she'll hold you in a vice-like grip. 1987 rating: she's got her claws into you!

A **Taurus husband** is a solid family man, proud of his home, wife and kids. He becomes a weighty man, whereas you like to feel free as air. 1987 rating: too steady by half.

A **Taurus wife** is the salt of the earth – always food on the table, wood in the fire! You make the marriage tick, she makes it run. 1987 rating: you take her too much for granted.

With a **Taurus boss** you can work smoothly on routine work; but you think he's unadventurous. 1987 rating: not the year to get closer. It's a so-so relationship.

Gemini

May 22 to June 21

Friendship Geminians are the most friendly people in the Zodiac, though, to be honest, they are better at making casual acquaintances than deep personal ties. One reason is that people find them an attractive type, easy to be with, because they have the gift of adapting themselves to suit the company. But they are fair-weather friends. If trouble looms, they don't want to know.

Sex Gemini people talk themselves into and out of love, almost as though it were a game. Gemini is not a highly-sexed sign, even though they may have plenty of sexual experience. Instead, sex for them is a rather special form of conversation. It does not necessarily involve them in deep feelings. But it's quite possible for Geminians to enjoy non-sexual relationships.

Marriage As Gemini is the most devious, two-faced and free-wheeling of all Zodiac signs, it follows that marriage is not really suited to their nature. But they can still make a success of marriage. They need a partner who can keep them on their toes; who can spring surprises; who is more a lover than a spouse; and who, if necessary, can turn a blind eye every time they stray.

Gemini (May 22 to June 21) and You

You form an entertaining relationship apt to fall apart. You are not desperately loyal, and may go your separate ways.

A **Gemini friend** is like a brother, almost a twin. You see the world in the same way. You tend to like fashion, change, new stimuli all the time. 1987 rating: very vivacious.

If you have a **Gemini parent** there will be many happy days

14

together. You see the world through the same eyes. Never much of a generation gap here. 1987 rating: warm and friendly.

With a **Gemini child** there's a similar air of well-being and happiness. This child should be a wonderful communicator, and will make you proud. 1987 rating: lots of fun together.

A **Gemini boy-friend** is more like a sexy brother than a real lover. This is fun at first, but may be ultimately unsatisfying. 1987 rating: he won't stay faithful, given half a chance.

With a **Gemini girl-friend** you can have a lively, inventive relationship at best. At worst, it's a nervy kind of union. 1987 rating: terrific to start with. Big effort after that.

A **Gemini husband** is a sociable type like yourself. You have many interests outside the home and family. Both of you need emotional space. 1987 rating: he's subtly changing.

A **Gemini wife** is a friendly creature, caught up in her own interests. You have plenty to talk about, but do you share much of an emotional life? 1987 rating: better than last year.

If you have a **Gemini boss** you will enjoy your working hours together, but others won't be so amused. 1987 rating: average to good, especially if you've just started working together.

Cancer

June 22 to July 22

Friendship Cancerians are clannish people at the best of times. They want to be friendly, but they can't help being suspicious of strangers at first. Once they've decided to make someone a friend, they tend to adopt them completely, drawing them into the family, so to speak. Cancerians have a great ability to identify with their friends' feelings, and love sharing.

Sex Although shy at first, Cancer folk soon fall hook, line and sinker for the right sweetheart. They're terrible clingers, hanging on for dear life if a lover seems to be losing interest. Sexually they have access to deep, ecstatic feelings. Physical pleasure is nothing

15

compared with the spiritual orgasms they are capable of experiencing. Cancerians never forget a former sweetheart, and still feel possessive after many years.

Marriage Cancerians are born to be married. They want to share their life with the perfect partner. Cancer men have a good deal of tenderness in their natures; they like strong-minded women who will look after them – indeed, mother them. Cancer women are very feminine, and need men who are kind, loyal and humorous – in short, a homely chap. All Cancerians love their family ties.

Cancer (June 22 to July 22) and You

You are very different people. You are versatile, clever, two-faced – while Cancer is heartfelt, sentimental and sincere.

A **Cancer friend** is loyal, emotional and much more possessive than you. He or she takes your casual remarks to heart, so beware of wounding remarks. 1987 rating: you're good together.

With a **Cancer parent** you have a safe, kindly, sometimes over-emotional person who is sometimes too cautious for your liking. 1987 rating: you're bored, and look for other company.

Towards a **Cancer child** you'll be rather impatient at times. He or she feels life much more deeply than you. Sometimes you can seem too shallow and uncaring. 1987 rating: pleasant.

A **Cancer boy-friend** desperately wants to be liked. You can find in him much that you lack in yourself. Beware of silly moods at times. 1987 rating: highly sexy.

A **Cancer girl-friend** enjoys emotional drama, so it's an on-and-off relationship. You're both highly-strung. She will mother you – and smother you. 1987 rating: good at times.

A **Cancer husband** will try to pin you down to a life of kids and soap-powder. Or else he'll do all the household tasks himself. 1987 rating: he's stuck in a rut, so you think.

A **Cancer wife** will look after you so well that in a subtle way she'll prevent you from truly growing up. You can learn much from each other. 1987 rating: much smoother.

If you have a **Cancer boss** there will be a good relationship most of the time. 1987 rating: good fun together, but your ideas won't always be appreciated.

Leo

July 23 to August 23

Friendship All Leo folk thrive on friendship, but Leo likes to be the dominant partner. They want to be flattered, praised, loved and enjoyed – that's what friendship means to them. But that isn't all. For a Leo, the heart will always rule the head. They would do anything for a friend – indeed, they would put friendship above all.

Sex There's only one thing to do on a hot afternoon – and that is to make love! So think Leo people, anyway. Nothing pleases them more than someone of the opposite sex making eyes at them. They love to be wooed. Falling in love comes very naturally to Leo folk. It's probably true to say that a Leo can't feel truly fulfilled without a good sex life.

Marriage Leos may enjoy flirting at parties, but in the end they are looking for a steady marriage. They need courtship and security at the same time. If ever a marriage breaks up, it can shatter the Leo heart – and like a broken mirror it never quite recovers. A Leo man needs a warmly responsive wife, while the Leo woman wants fidelity and affection.

Leo (July 23 to August 23) and You

One of the most successful Zodiac partnerships. You keep each other alive and alert without getting on each other's nerves.

A **Leo friend** is a mixture of warmth and bluster. You get on well, provided you don't tease too much. Leo wants to take the lead. 1987 rating: clashes of pride. Learn to relax.

If you have a **Leo parent** you should get on marvellously well.

17

You lift each other's spirits, though sometimes you'll be bossed around too much. 1987 rating: mature and interesting.

With a **Leo child** you have someone whom you constantly want to push into the limelight. You have lots of pride in his or her success. 1987 rating: good times together.

A **Leo boy-friend** has lots of sexual compatability with you. You're just the kind of flirt he likes. This is a warm, sociable, extrovert relationship. 1987 rating: smashing!

A relationship with a **Leo girl-friend** is likely to be a light-hearted liaison. You don't take each other too seriously, but can be desperately in love. 1987 rating: wedding bells?

A **Leo husband** will make a good marriage partner. You'll be popular with neighbours. The marriage thrives on success, not on failure. 1987 rating: someone will think of straying.

With a **Leo wife** you make a smart pair, keen to get on and know all the right people. Not desperately keen on kids, as you like to stay young yourselves. 1987 rating: restless.

A **Leo boss** is fun to be with. You just flatter him to get what you want. 1987 rating: good in a hi-tech, modern industry. In an old-fashioned job, you'll gradually hate each other.

Virgo

August 24 to September 22

Friendship Virgo people distrust strangers. When they meet a new person, they're distant at first. Only when they feel safe will they relax and become more personal. Even then, they are not as friendly as most Zodiac signs. They don't mix as freely, and are much more choosy about friends. They like people who are kindly, intelligent and observant – like themselves.

Sex Traditionally Virgo is the least sexy of all the Zodiac. Virgo people are capable of strong platonic friendships, and they don't seem to need sex as much as other people. Perhaps they need awakening – and once they realise how exciting it can be, they enjoy a splendid sex life. Some Virgoans, particularly women, put themselves on a pedestal, pretending to be far too good for the opposite sex.

Marriage Virgoans tend to remain unmarried longer than other signs. They need space to themselves, where they can be private. Virgoan men need a strong-minded wife who won't be too domineering. He needs someone who will give him enthusiasm as well as encouragement. Virgoan women look for emotional security. They are the kind to have a career outside marriage.

Virgo (August 24 to September 22) and You

Both are ruled by Mercury, but there the similarity ends. It's a clever relationship – sometimes too clever and self-aware.

A **Virgo friend** is a bit pernickety, and isn't as warm and open as you. A good friendship for sharing ideas. Virgo is more private than you. 1987 rating: sensible and charitable.

A **Virgo parent** will have given you a pleasant upbringing, though may have thought you were too untidy and slapdash. 1987 rating: when quarrels start, count to ten.

With a **Virgo child** you are inclined to be too devil-may-care. Remember that Virgo children need plenty of steady routine. 1987 rating: warmer than in recent years.

A **Virgo boy-friend** can be shy at first, and may always seem a bit reserved and self-contained. You're a bright, nervy couple. 1987 rating: give it time. There's a lot of hope.

A **Virgo girl-friend** is friendly, but a bit of a prude. Both of you enjoy mental companionship as much as passion. She is not really a sharer. 1987 rating: nervy and restless.

A **Virgo husband** is conscientious, and a good bread-winner, but a lot more conventional than you. You may outgrow him. 1987 rating: you seem to want different things out of life.

A **Virgo wife** is honest and decent, a good housewife but keen to keep improving her mind. You make a well-matched couple. 1987 rating: trouble in the family circle.

A **Virgo boss** is a fair employer, unless he feels that you are taking advantage of him. 1987 rating: be punctual and efficient, and there'll be no complaints.

Libra

September 23 to October 23

Friendship Librans thrive on friendship – more than any other Zodiac sign. Without friends they feel lost, only half-alive, for they are so amicable themselves. They mix easily, but can quickly detect if someone is 'not nice'. They adore small talk, chats on the phone, and social gatherings of all kinds. They have the rare ability to stay in touch with childhood friends.

Sex Librans are made for loving! They are one of those Zodiac signs who do distinguish between sex and love. Love without sex is okay, but sex without love is abhorrent. In the right relationship, they want to share themselves, body and soul, with the person they love. They are the psychological type who is drawn to their opposite – not always a good thing!

Marriage Of all Zodiac signs, Libra is the one most suited to marriage. They seem to be born as 'twin souls', and spend their lives looking for the ideal mate. Librans of both sexes need someone who is a good pal as well as lover. Libran men need an organised woman who isn't bossy. Libran women feel they need a real macho man who will look after them forever.

Libra (September 23 to October 23) and You

A friendly, affable affair lacking solidity and firmness. Good in the company of others. Good rapport – for a while.

A **Libra friend** is a charmer and no mistake. You have a great deal to talk about, so it's a gossipy little friendship. One of the best links in the Zodiac. 1987 rating: warm-hearted.

With a **Libra parent** there will be lots of happiness. This is the parent who understands you best. Other members of the family will envy your rapport. 1987 rating: excellent.

If you have a **Libra child** you will delight in his or her cute little ways. There's always a flow of tenderness between you. 1987 rating: lots to be proud of.

A **Libra boy-friend** is kind, loving – and rather a womaniser! It's the sweet nothings in the ear that turn you on. Don't expect a quick proposal, though. 1987 rating: you take the lead.

A **Libra girl-friend** suits you, so there's lots of fondness. She understands your outlook on life, and is an ideal partner. 1987 rating: be stimulating company to each other.

A **Libra husband** is indecisive at times. Your mind is quick and restless in comparison, but this should still be a good marriage. 1987 rating: job changes mean a change of outlook.

With a **Libra wife** you form a sweet couple, out-and-about more than stay-at-home. You keep each other young and happy. Very good with children. 1987 rating: she's more pushy than usual.

With a **Libra boss** you have plenty of compatability – inside and outside working hours. 1987 rating: an easy relationship, though you'll take more and more charge of events!

Scorpio

October 24 to November 22

Friendship Scorpio people are highly suspicious of newcomers. They don't make friends easily, and they can test their friendships so severely that they frighten would-be pals away. But once a true friendship is formed, it lasts for life. As far as Scorpio is concerned, friendship is a matter of utter loyalty. Friendship with members of their own sex is very important.

Sex Sex is a deeper, richer experience for Scorpio than perhaps for anyone else. At the same time, they manage to make sex far more complex and meaningful than it need be. Many Scorpians are frightened of sexual power. Raw sex, without love, worries them

21

more than most people. It's certainly hard for them to have a casual, lightweight affair. As in so many other aspects of their lives, it's all or nothing.

Marriage Scorpians don't take their marriage vows lightly. They mean to keep them, through bad times as well as good. They can be very jealous if slighted, but within a happy relationship they are the happiest of partners, for they are capable of much devotion. Scorpio men need a woman who can be a real soul-mate. Scorpio women need a strong man – the tougher the better.

Scorpio (October 24 to November 22) **and You**

A love-hate relationship! Each admires and despises the other. Rarely a sedate union, but you can learn plenty from each other.

A **Scorpio friend** can be fascinating company, but Scorpio can also be moody and a little cruel. The friendship must be deep, or it's nothing. 1987 rating: some silent disagreements.

A **Scorpio parent** is someone you can't help admiring and disliking! There's a strong willpower that you lack, but also secrecy and emotional reserve. 1987 rating: edgy.

A **Scorpio child** keeps himself to himself. He isn't nearly as open and gossipy as yourself. Always encourage him to be positive. 1987 rating: careful guidance needed.

A **Scorpio boy-friend** sees you as a butterfly he can capture and make his own. He expects plenty of you. Not compatible, but you can still be attracted. 1987 rating: brooding and moody.

A **Scorpio girl-friend** needs a real man – not an unreliable jokey type like yourself! You may feel she's too serious and clinging for you. 1987 rating: lots of romance.

A **Scorpio husband** may be too solemn for a lifetime with you. He may not give you the freedom and flexibility you need. 1987 rating: pleasant time, after some tension in 1986.

A **Scorpio wife** is not really suited. She'll find you too lightweight, and you'll think she's jealous and possessive. 1987 rating: your spare-time hobbies take you apart.

A **Scorpio boss** will be a difficult creature to cope with. I doubt whether working life is easy. 1987 rating: pleasant at first, but disagreements gradually developing.

Sagittarius

November 23 to December 21

Friendship Sagittarians are friendly – for a while – but people cannot rely on them. They can drop friends as easily as they can pick them up – without much heartbreak. Most Sagittarians have a built-in charm that never fails to attract. There's a relaxed, informal manner which doesn't really look for lasting links. They like new people, so old pals are taken for granted.

Sex They have a very flirtatious manner that enjoys chatting up the opposite sex. There's also an element of victory involved. They like to win hearts, and at times they get a thrill from leaving a broken heart by the wayside. Sagittarians enjoy sex on impulse, perhaps in exotic locations! They can get bored with the sameness of love-making with the same old partner!

Marriage Sagittarians are not the most monogamous of people. It's hard for them to maintain interest in one person all their lives, so they need partners who have the same variety-seeking outlook on life that Sagittarians have. Men born under Sagittarius appreciate a woman with a mind of her own. Sagittarian women respond to real men, full of zest for life.

Sagittarius (November 23 to December 21) and You

So similar, so different! Both of you are talkative, adventurous and untraditional. Very suitable, but you may drift apart.

A **Sagittarius friend** is an admirable pal – the ideal foil to your wit. Sagittarius is the best friendship in the whole Zodiac for you. 1987 rating: you are competitive.

With a **Sagittarius parent** you have had a lot of fun. This is a lively, free-and-easy relationship which can always recover from

23

cross moments. 1987 rating: temper and high spirits.

With a **Sagittarius child** there will be arguments which you both enjoy. Encourage sport and studies. This child will leave home early. 1987 rating: good for sport.

A **Sagittarius boy-friend** is marvellous as a lover – a real hero but never heavy-handed. He likes your sense of fun and adventure. 1987 rating: sexy, but it could suddenly break up.

A **Sagittarius girl-friend** responds to impulse and experiment. You can stimulate each other in many ways, but equally can get bored quickly. 1987 rating: she's looking for security.

A **Sagittarius husband** is an excellent choice of mate. He likes variety in life, and so do you – perhaps you'll travel together. 1987 rating: he's looking for an adventure.

With a **Sagittarius wife** you'll have an easy-going marriage, without many hassles. Whether you'll stay loyal to each other is another matter. 1987 rating: a clash, then much warmer.

A **Sagittarius boss** can be full of hare-brained schemes. You'll go along with them. 1987 rating: charming and positive. You should enjoy working together.

Capricorn

December 22 to January 20

Friendship Capricorn folk make friends with difficulty – but once made, they tend to remain friends for life. The wall around the Capricorn heart makes it hard for us to get to know them well. Friendship for the Capricorn type is not a light-hearted, take-it-or-leave-it affair. It must be based on real virtues such as trust, honour and the readiness to help.

Sex Capricorn people have such a cold manner at times that they appear unsexy. Actually they are highly sexed, though it does not always flow out in a harmonious way. They are not flirty types. They adopt a serious approach to life, and can turn nasty and jealous if slighted. Yet their planet Saturn is linked to the old Roman orgies, so they can certainly let themselves go! They can turn from frost to warmth in a split second!

Marriage Marriage is a solemn matter to Capricorn folk. They intend to make it last for life. Once married, they feel they own their partners. They don't look for freedom or adventure. All their energies are devoted to maintaining the marriage as it is. This can lead to a stale situation where they take their spouses too much for granted.

Capricorn (December 22 to January 20) and You

Meant to be poles apart, but actually you get on well together. You hate the Capricorn stodginess, but respect the commonsense.

A **Capricorn friend** can be heavy going. Capricorn is much more of a worrier than you. Meant to be poles apart, you can actually complement each other. 1987 rating: splendid.

A **Capricorn parent** is a careful, serious-minded type who may have restricted you in your younger days. Don't let your fun be snuffed out. 1987 rating: better links nowadays.

A **Capricorn child** is following a steady groove in life. Don't stir things up unnecessarily. Be full of encouragement. 1987 rating: amiable, if there's plenty of tolerance.

A **Capricorn boy-friend** won't get involved until he's sure it's the right thing to do. Then he will get ten out of ten for effort! 1987 rating: irritation plus fondness.

A **Capricorn girl-friend** wants a man who'll treat her like a lady. You're too fly, too sly for that! So she may not take you seriously. 1987 rating: good fun, but seriousness too.

A **Capricorn husband** is the sort of chap who tells you what TV programmes to watch. Okay if you want to marry a father-figure. 1987 rating: you'll be struggling.

A **Capricorn wife** will give you discipline, and urge you to be ambitious – and want to be a career woman herself. A tower of strength in a crisis. 1987 rating: excellent.

A **Capricorn boss**, meanwhile, will be a stern task-master, and won't stand much nonsense from you. 1987 rating: relationship depends on working conditions.

Aquarius

January 21 to February 18

Friendship Friendships mean much to Aquarians. At the same time they want to remain independent. So they are friendly with lots of people, but always slightly stand-offish – as if they are really on their own. Aquarians are good at making and keeping friends. Primarily they are interested in mental friendship – the rapport between people who share the same interests.

Sex Aquarius is one of three signs (Gemini and Virgo are the others) that are not obviously sexual. Don't worry, they can have a perfectly normal and happy love life; but they treat people as humans first, and as sexual partners only later. They are capable of great tenderness. But a passionate partner will say they don't get sufficiently involved.

Marriage Aquarians see their partners as equals – not people who must be dominated or obeyed. At the same time they're freedom-loving in outlook, so it's difficult for them to share the little things in life. They need emotional elbow-room, and hate to be owned or trapped. Aquarians are rarely the unhappy victims of marriage. If it breaks up, Aquarians are the first to go.

Aquarius (January 21 to February 18) and You

One of the best mixtures in the Zodiac. You can establish a quick mental rapport, but Aquarius has more stamina than you.

An **Aquarius friend** is a dry, odd-ball companion who may lead you a merry dance. You're both individualists, so should get on well. 1987 rating: an inquisitive relationship.

An **Aquarius parent** is just the kind of Mum or Dad you needed. You don't interfere too much in each other's lives. Lots of

26

friendly discussions. 1987 rating: plenty of emotional space.

With an **Aquarius child** humour is always the saving grace between you. You can establish a quick, intelligent rapport. 1987 rating: you share many interests.

An **Aquarius boy-friend** can be cool to the point of coldness. To him, sex is a way of saying 'hello'. To you, it's a way of saying 'goodbye'. 1987 rating: clever, but sexy too.

An **Aquarius girl-friend** can provide a great sense of fellow-feeling – but the sexuality can ooze away into pecks on the cheek. 1987 rating: she's a bit of a nut case!

An **Aquarius husband** is a bit stand-offish, but he certainly gives you the freedom to be yourself, which is nice. You're a cool, modern couple. 1987 rating: lots of compatability.

With an **Aquarius wife** you make a striking couple, always lively and nonconformist. You may not be mad-keen on children. 1987 rating: more money means a happier relationship.

If you have an **Aquarius boss** you could be a brilliantly inventive team. 1987 rating: you work well together in health, education, law – poorly in industry or commerce.

Pisces

February 19 to March 20

Friendship Pisceans are friendly folk. They enjoy meeting new people and can quickly become dependent on new friends – for love, loyalty and, if need be, support if things go wrong. At the same time they don't like to be 'owned', and get frustrated if chums try to organise their lives too much. Piscean men relate well to women, but Piscean women may be in awe of clever male friends.

Sex The Piscean aim in love is to achieve a wonderful, yielding rapport with their partners. They want to melt into love-making, losing their own identity. All the same, Pisceans are fussy in choosing the right partner. Because their imagination is powerful,

27

they can see a would-be sexual partner in a rosy-coloured light, and can be terribly let down later. Sex without love does not suit the Piscean at all.

Marriage Pisceans have an ambiguous attitude towards marriage. In one way, their whole impulse is to make someone else happy and fulfilled. At the same time, they need to feel free. They should not marry someone who will be too possessive. Piscean men look for a woman who will take the lead in the marriage. Piscean women can be misused by an over-dominant husband.

Pisces (February 19 to March 20) and You

You seem magnificently well-matched, but in your private lives there can be tension. Pisces is so vague compared with you.

A **Pisces friend** seems well-matched on the surface, but there can be hidden tensions. You respect facts: Pisces responds to feelings. 1987 rating: irritated with each other at times.

A **Pisces parent** may be forgetful and dithery in your eyes, but there's still lots of love between you. 1987 rating: there may be a major disagreement over living arrangements.

A **Pisces child** is full of love – but he or she is a sensitive flower, and mustn't be disciplined too much. Expect this child to be unpunctual. 1987 rating: a floaty, escapist time.

A **Pisces boy-friend** is not very reliable – but then, nor are you! Very sexy in short bursts. Have fun together! 1987 rating: you can't trust him completely.

A **Pisces girl-friend** needs to be wooed with sweet talk – something you're good at! She'll cling more than you like. 1987 rating: some cross words, but love underneath.

With a **Pisces husband** you can be tender and loving, but the marriage lacks direction and drive at times. Lots of little white lies! 1987 rating: someone is being devious.

A **Pisces wife** lives in a dream-world of her own which annoys you at times. Try to be patient and tolerant. She's wonderful with the children. 1987 rating: not an easy year together.

From a **Pisces boss** you receive affection – but may not know where you stand. 1987 rating: he may take advantage of your good nature.

Birthday

Message

This book applies to everyone born between
May 22 and June 21. But here, just for you,
is a special word of hope or caution,
depending on your actual birthday in Gemini.
Here is your own astrological message
to guide you through the year ahead.

MAY

Friday 22nd: A serious-minded year. You have the initiative to get what you want – but at a price. Expect some alarms and surprises in your love life!

Saturday 23rd: You may want to break free from conditions that are cramping your style. It's an excellent year for dreaming great dreams – and maybe seeing one come true.

Sunday 24th: A free-n-easy year, but there may be one drawback to your plans. Travel seems likely. One relationship will pass through a tense phase.

Monday 25th: A positive and encouraging year. Don't raise your hopes too high. You may kiss one person goodbye, only to find someone else waiting for you.

Tuesday 26th: A restless year. Even if you're happy, you won't be satisfied! A little illness will make you work harder than ever once you're well again. Could be promotion.

Wednesday 27th: A lucky year in some ways. You are probably on the move. Romantic life has a few surprises, but you'll end up happier. Finances could improve dramatically.

Thursday 28th: Quite a hard-pressed 1987, but you should enjoy a lucky streak as well – in love, money or both. There may be nice news from abroad.

29

Friday 29th: Slight ait of muddle this year. Maybe you don't want to know the truth. You will feel taken to the end of your tether, but there's better news to come.

Saturday 30th: There's a shifting of gears in your life. You'll start to move faster in a clearcut direction. You will be less in the hands of others.

Sunday 31st: A happy year for home and family – especially for new additions. There's a slight battle between head and heart. In the end you'll follow your commonsense.

JUNE

Monday 1st: Some financial hardship. You may feel that your efforts are not appreciated. Good year for encouraging the rest of the family. Your Geminian communicative skills are valued.

Tuesday 2nd: Money doesn't materialise as quickly as you want. You will be rid of one long-standing problem – after a battle. You are prone to illness, so stay as robust as possible.

Wednesday 3rd: A hard-working year, but not in pleasant circumstances. After a period of strain, love will flow again. You will feel sorry for one relative in particular.

Thursday 4th: Quite a jolly year. You may have more than one admirer. Some aggro to handle within the family circle. Parents may interfere too much. You'll work hard.

Friday 5th: There's a feeling of life slipping by, without a great deal to show for it. It's too easy for you to abandon hope. Try to develop more fight and spirit.

Saturday 6th: A better year. You seem to be firing on all cylinders. People will appreciate your efforts. A complex money plan will eventually work out well.

Sunday 7th: Your love life seems slightly topsy-turvy. Perhaps you can't trust your partner as you'd like. More probably, you are the one who is untrustworthy!

Monday 8th: Reality catches up with you. You won't be able to get away with a trick or lie any more. Quite an expansive year, so your horizons are broadening.

Tuesday 9th: If you're unhappy, you'll see a way of freeing yourself. It pays to be more self-oriented for a while. Family matters can look after themselves.

Wednesday 10th: An effortful year, especially around your birthday. You will feel you aren't getting the lucky breaks. A year for gritting the teeth and keeping on keeping on.

Thursday 11th: An energetic year, with hostility around you. You may lose some friends, as you're no pushover right now. A good year to start a business or meet a new partner.

Friday 12th: Lots of energy at your disposal. Don't fritter it away. Excellent time to start a new job. Sadly you may have a new enemy to deal with.

Saturday 13th: Fairly easy year so long as you are working. If you're unemployed, you will have too much frustration to be truly happy. Lots of anger hovering on the sidelines.

Sunday 14th: Quite a lucky year. You seem to be basking in the sunlight of success. A change should be for the better. It's who you know that counts.

Monday 15th: A much better year. You seem well off, and will enjoy spending. It's the right year to make a fundamental break with the past. Lots of energy and drive.

Tuesday 16th: You could enter a much happier phase of life, but it means a radical change in outlook and circumstances. You'll act on impulse instead of carefully laid plans.

Wednesday 17th: Your life could change startlingly in the next twelve months. Don't say no to experiment. You will put your love life on a new footing.

Thursday 18th: You can't quite do what you want, though you feel like breaking out of a rut. Your love life could reach the point of no return. Basically a lucky time, though.

Friday 19th: You may make heavy weather of your problems. It's a time for growing up and accepting the responsibilities ahead. You seem luckier in love than in career.

Saturday 20th: Quite a hard slog in the months ahead, but you will have something positive to show for your efforts. There's one extremely lucky influence helping you.

Sunday 21st: You'll feel trapped by circumstances. Good time to settle down with home and family. One bright idea could make a big change to your working arrangements.

Your Year

Ahead

You start the year in better shape than most people. You are energetic, hard-working and purposive. Financially you do quite well, with some luck and perhaps a lump sum coming your way. February looks restless, even irritable. Your work looks changeable, and there could be some trouble with the people you live with. Any new sweetheart will be loving and giving – too good for you, anyway!

Family history starts to intrigue you in March. There may also be talk of a pay rise. You have to worry about the welfare of an elderly relative.

April looks more amiable. You may take a holiday with another family, and enjoy yourself enormously. There could be thoughts of marriage, especially with someone older than yourself.

If work and home life have been rather a prison for you, May is the time to break free. It's a happy, adventurous time, best if you're single and fancy-free.

June, too, looks relaxed and loving. It's a good time to be training for some new aspect of work. Children do well, and your own leisure life is full to bursting.

July looks more mixed-up. Someone may have hurt you, and now you want to get your own back. There could be some infidelity in your life. August is also a rougher, tougher time. The self-confidence which has kept you merry and bright starts to turn a little sour.

Any arguments will continue into September, when you're trying for too much too soon. You could land a super new job, though. October is more constructive, and you're worried about your long-term future. A difficult month in love. November looks much the same, but you should enjoy the closing stages of 1987. You'll be looking forward to the challenge of 1988.

New-born Geminians will be bright, alert and noisy for most of the time. They enjoy being noticed, and have a fine sense of humour from an early age. No great problems this year – they look healthy and intelligent.

Gemini **youngsters** are in a tearaway mood. They are not very obedient at the moment, and can be easily influenced by older children. Being naturally clever, they should do well in exams, but they're wonderful at making excuses if they fail!

Elderly Geminians face a broadly optimistic year, though the middle months will be a shade boring. No special problems with health, and day-to-day expenses look as though they'll be okay.

If you are **chronically ill** there is a definite chance of recovery in the first half of the year. Paralysis and stiffness are both liable to ease. The more you can stay active, the fitter you'll be – and the easier you can keep wasting diseases like cancer at bay.

Out-of-work Geminians have two excellent chances of finding the right job this coming year: the first in January-February, the second in mid-1987. You need a job where you can use your charm and sociability.

If you **run your own business** the first half of 1987 is a great time for expanding the range of your services. Sales could rocket up. It's also a terrific moment to be launching a new career for yourself.

If the last few months – or years – have been **lonely**, you have quite a success in early 1987, though the passion may not last. I think it's more likely that you'll have two sweet-hearts than one, and won't want to choose between them.

Geminians who have a **rocky marriage** should find the relationship improving in 1987. If it doesn't, you may not end it straight away, but will certainly turn it into an open marriage.

If you are planning to **move** there are good signs for 1987. The new home will need some alterations, but you'll be very happy there – eventually. You may have to put up with temporary accommodation for a while, though.

January

Guide

You start the year in better heart than most people. The first half of January looks energetic, hard-working and opportunistic. The second half is more floaty, with plans uncertain. Perhaps you'll have several balloons in the air at the same time, and it will take all your Geminian dexterity to keep them aloft!

Your best time seems to be the second week, when you should be extra-lively, full of bright ideas and eager to get on with life. Very exciting.

There may be a problem over a group of friends who are giving you a hard time. There may be extra responsibilities which you only half-welcome. If you work for a voluntary organisation, for instance, there could be administrative or money worries.

WORK. You make a useful start to the working year. If you are unemployed at present, there's a good chance of landing a new job in the first week of January.

If you have a steady job, there will be a new routine that suits you. A part-time job could soon yield extra hours.

Colleagues at work are not all that helpful, however. If you are competing with one person, I'm not sure you will win.

If you have a difficult immediate boss, expect a bad mood between you in the second and third weeks.

HOME. Fairly peaceable time, though you may not see as much of each other as you normally do. One member of the household may be departing for far-off shores. If you have a relative working abroad, there will be news of promotion.

There could be more contact than usual with older relatives. You may feel you haven't spent enough time with grandparents, for instance. If you are responsible for the welfare of any older

34

relatives, you will be turning your mind over some new possibilities – including an eventual move of home.

HEALTH. Quite a robust month. You have a better chance than most of surviving viruses, etc.

There could be a slight kidney disorder during the second week. It's unlikely to be serious, but could lead to inflammation and discomfort.

It's also a time to beware casual sex encounters. Around 10th to 16th you are susceptible to sexually transmitted infections.

MONEY. Financially 1987 starts better than expected. There could be a lump sum coming your way – perhaps one that you've half-forgotten about.

It's a good moment to straighten your finances, especially if you're a chronic late payer. It's to your advantage to use one of your bank's easy-payment schemes for regular expenses such as rent, rates and the utilities. You'll find it much more comfortable in the long run.

There are several lucky moments this month. There could be a special event in the news that attracts betting: a royal baby announcement, say, or the date of the next election. You will be luckier than most in this sort of wager.

LEISURE. Not a brilliant month for leisure activities. Perhaps you will have enjoyed yourself too much over the Christmas hols to spare much energy for more fun in January.

If you play a musical instrument, there may be a special reason for practising harder this month. Perhaps you'll be taking part in a performance soon. The same applies if you're a singer.

Watch out for a new friend whom you meet via the family, and also an old friend who has fallen on hard times. You'll want to give practical help, if possible.

LOVE. Not a sparkling month for love, but not terrible either! Your own sex drive is average to good, but partners or would-be partners are not so enthusiastic.

There could be one person paying you a good deal of attention, but I get the feeling that you're not very interested.

Within a steady relationship there could be numerous small bickerings and criticisms that spoil the flow of true love.

January

Key Dates

Thursday 1st: *Slightly at sixes and sevens. A friendly row may turn into an open quarrel.* You may appear too clever by half. Try to help a youngster in distress.

Friday 2nd: *Muddled time. Lies will be told. But warm-hearted too, so perhaps a reconciliation.* You can talk your way into someone's affections – but do you really mean it?

Saturday 3rd: *Still an air of deceit. Information is unreliable. The family has something to celebrate.* You could make a long journey on someone else's behalf.

Sunday 4th: *A sexy weekend. Older people are appreciated. But one group of people are stubborn.* A happy time provided you can contact the right people in the time. Good links with Leos.

Monday 5th: *Lots of striving for success. An agreement could be reached.* Good time for business meetings. If health has been troublesome, you'll heave a sigh of relief.

Tuesday 6th: *Serious working day. Still a happy time for those in love.* There could be a pleasant romantic encounter. Someone new could be paying special attention to you.

Wednesday 7th: *A row breaks out between members of a group. Old heads are wiser than young hearts.* You'll be annoyed if someone keeps changing his or her mind – but so do you!

Thursday 8th: *Minor criticisms spoil the overall mood. Folk are out of sorts with each other.* You seem happier than most, with something definite to aim for. Lucky time: afternoon.

Friday 9th: *More cheerful day or two, but arguments still break out.* A half-baked idea will soon take firmer shape. There's an air of anticipation in your life.

Saturday 10th: *Good news for some. Still not a restful time for the world.* An enjoyable weekend. You hear good news from friends or family. You may be the life and soul of a party.

Sunday 11th: *Good weekend for travel. A little white lie saves trouble!* Beware of letting slip a secret you promised to keep to yourself! Nice day for reading, writing, paying bills.

Monday 12th: *Good for talks, negotiations, deals – but some folk are out to make trouble.* You could make a fool of yourself by not knowing the full facts. Step warily in the company of men.

Tuesday 13th: *Lively, restless time with many small changes in the offing.* There's exciting news to pass on. You can act as B, putting A in touch with C. Lucky colour: red.

Wednesday 14th: *Still restless. A new idea could solve an old problem.* Nice evening to go out with a group of friends. Any regular meeting will have a touch of glamour tonight.

Thursday 15th: *Nothing goes quite to plan. The bright ideas are still favoured.* You may feel you're kept waiting by others. A repair job will take longer than expected.

Friday 16th: *Unsettled day. Perhaps there's the promise of more difficulties to come.* You could be exasperated by delays. Use the phone to keep people on their toes.

Saturday 17th: *A weekend when feelings get out of hand. There's some deception afoot.* You may be skating on thin ice, where a relationship is concerned. A chance meeting could be awkward.

Sunday 18th: *Reality catches up with those who have gone astray. Perhaps an escape comes to nothing.* You may have to tell several lies to get out of a tricky spot.

Monday 19th: *Still quite a grim scene. Imagination is getting the better of commonsense.* You seem in the hands of others. It could be a matter of crossing your fingers and hoping...

Tuesday 20th: *A way is found out of one difficulty. A dogged day.* You'll easily get bored, and may leave jobs unfinished. A competitor may over-take you.

Wednesday 21st: *More friendly – also more devious! Outsiders are given a chance.* You'd like to take a risk, but you're doubtful of success. Better to hesitate than take the wrong action.

Thursday 22nd: *A calming influence. The rough and tumble of the last few days gives way to peace.* Things work out better than expected. There's plenty of catching up needed.

Friday 23rd: *Quarrels are patched up or forgotten. Better for women than men.* Gemini males may feel neglected. Gemini women get a surprising offer out of the blue.

Saturday 24th: *A sober weekend. Duty must be followed instead of pleasure.* Good time to work hard at a hobby or craft. A much older or younger person will take up your time.

Sunday 25th: *Low spirits for a while. There could be a delay or disappointment.* A meeting could be cancelled. A normally lively scene may be dead as the dodo. Something mechanical goes wrong.

Monday 26th: *More cheerful. Luck's in the air. There's a silver lining to that cloud!* You can turn nothing into something! A happy day, once you can see your way out of difficulties.

Tuesday 27th: *Still cheerful. Good time to force through a deal. But there's one area of doubt.* A difficult partner could be a pain in the neck. There could be a row with a youngster.

Wednesday 28th: *Careful day. People are on their best behaviour. An air of optimism.* There's a lot of instant fun. Good day to pick for a night out. You must pay more than your fair share.

Thursday 29th: *An extravagant time. If in doubt, spend! A great time to make new friends.* You'll enjoy window-shopping. Beware of impulse buying, though – you'll be sorry later.

Friday 30th: *If there's an obstacle, break it down! Not a day for half-measures!* Someone in your life gets very angry, and you must calm things down.

Saturday 31st: *Energetic time. Real feelings will burst out. A surprise for many folk.* You should be able to forget worries for a while. Good day for travel.

Wise Words for January

It's only damned fools who argue.
Never contradict, never explain, never apologise.
These are the secrets of a happy life.
Lord Fisher

February

Guide

Quite a restless month. Ideally you'll get away from your usual haunts during any spare time. A short holiday or a couple of day trips will do you the world of good.

You'll be restless in other ways — perhaps irritable is a better word. You won't suffer fools gladly, and if there's an imbalance in your marriage, there'll be a tendency for you to take it out on your spouse.

Quite an artistic month, too. You will want to express your taste in interior decor, clothes or maybe in some work of art.

Finally, you should enjoy the company of someone new. If this annoys anyone else, you won't be too bothered. It's a month when you want to please yourself.

WORK. Even in a humdrum job there will be an element of surprise and change. New equipment in a factory, fresh layout of a shop floor, different routines to follow — whatever the cause, the effect on you will be electric but also a bit depressive. You may work too hard, or worry too much about results. You will need more time to relax.

Mostly your work is straightforward and a little boring. You aren't expecting to get a big thrill out of it.

You will be under some pressure at work. For part of February your schedule will be easy going. Then suddenly there's a flurry of activity. If yours is a seasonal job, you'll find yourself working overtime.

HOME. Domestic life will be much affected by the relationship with the person you live with. If there's trouble between you, home life will lack sense and savour.

Older relatives will occupy your thoughts. You may notice one member of the family — a parent, grandparent or aunt — is not as crisp and efficient as in the past. Your mind will shift ahead to start planning living arrangements in the future.

If you've recently had new windows, you'll be disappointed by the lack of workmanship involved.

HEALTH. The only signs of ill-health occur right at the end of the month, when you could have a queasy tummy. Too much rich food and drink won't agree with you. Anyway, away from home you could pick up a little bug.

Disabled Geminians may receive a special bit of luck soon. It may be a special government payment, or, more personally, you could benefit from someone else's gadget that gets passed on to you.

MONEY. If you're looking for easy money, there could be a chance of a quick profit in the first three weeks. You might get something free which you can then sell: something to do with holidays and travel, I think.

One warning: if you have recently gained money through any kind of entertainment or sport, the taxman will be after you.

LEISURE. Expect a spot of travel to be rearranged, especially if there is an industrial stoppage.

In more peaceful communities there will be an opportunity to enjoy some culture (especially a live concert). There could be an exhibition of work by an artist you know personally.

You will enjoy something competitive involving machinery. This could be a motor rally, gymnastics or something even more unusual.

Some time during this February you could be given a freebie - a free ticket to a public relations event, perhaps.

LOVE. A new sweetheart will be very sweet and loving, but maybe a little neurotic as well. Don't jump in at the deep end; you could find yourself emotionally out of your depth.

There's no necessity for this to be the case. If not, mid-February is lovely for romance. You seem warm and happy. (Some Geminians, briefly parted, may be back with their sweethearts quicker than they think.)

There could be some discord in a personal relationship. You won't see eye to eye, and you will somehow end up the loser.

Good links with other Geminians, by the way.

February

Key Dates

Sunday 1st: *A day of surprises and shocks. People are looking for something different.* You will work out how to tackle a complex task, especially if other people's permission is needed.

Monday 2nd: *Friendly time, with the accent on 'getting to know you.'* Excellent time for meetings, interviews, etc. Things work out reasonably well. Lucky colour: white or grey.

Tuesday 3rd: *Good working day. Plenty can be achieved. Youth and age co-operate nicely.* The people around you are happy, but you have an inner anxiety – all about nothing, I daresay.

Wednesday 4th: *Friendly within the family. Still a practical time.* Beware of darting from one Gemini activity to the next. Something goes wrong for the *nth* time – you'll replace it.

Thursday 5th: *People want something for nothing. A buzz of excitement in the air.* There will be a failure of communications. A mixed-up time, with someone's imagination getting out of hand.

Friday 6th: *People are slightly out-of-sorts with each other. An older person creates trouble.* One of your quieter days. You don't feel as extrovert as usual.

Saturday 7th: *Quite an explosive time. There could be a narrow escape.* Beware of saying the wrong thing. You may be shocked by a neighbour's behaviour. Lucky number: 2.

Sunday 8th: *Some anger and short temper, but it will soon blow over.* Someone you love gets in touch. Be smarmy if necessary, and keep your real views to yourself.

Monday 9th: *A sensible day, but there's plenty of imagination and sensitivity, too.* You must deal with someone who suffers a loss. Put on a sad face. The evening looks better.

Tuesday 10th: *Some aggro, but it sounds worse than it really is. Love tries to break out!* You may have to deal with someone who is drunk or ill-tempered. It could all end in laughs.

Wednesday 11th: *Plans could start to fall apart. You're unsure where you stand.* Perhaps you're getting a dose of your own medicine. If you've lied in the past, you'll be lied to now.

Thursday 12th: *You could be deceived by someone normally trustworthy.* It's unlikely to be a serious matter, but you'll feel let down. Rather a depressed day.

Friday 13th: *Pleasantly energetic time. A bright idea could solve everything.* You'll turn your mind to a fresh project, and get quickly enthusiastic about it.

Saturday 14th: *There's a new initiative. Expect a sudden breakthrough.* A couple of phone calls make you excited. Children will take up a lot of time. Lucky colour: red or orange.

Sunday 15th: *Pleasant weekend, but you need to tackle something energetic.* One group of friends will lead to new friends. You may unwittingly hurt an old friend's feelings.

Monday 16th: *You hear something intriguing. Still the promise of something unusual.* You don't feel like making a full contribution. Perhaps you are feeling slightly ill.

Tuesday 17th: *Quite lucky and extravagant and flirty – great for having fun.* You will make a quick recovery, and should be bouncy and full of vigour. Be lucky in late afternoon.

Wednesday 18th: *Good fun likely. People are in a who-cares mood. Loving and larky.* It's a wonderful time to flatter someone nice and handsome. You can revive a friendship that's languished.

Thursday 19th: *Not an organised day, but plenty gets done. A time to enjoy yourself.* A lovely surprise out of the blue. Make an early start. You may worry that a friend has gone off you.

Friday 20th: *Little arguments and minor alterations, but no big problems.* This promises to be an interesting day. You may meet a fascinating person. A do-it-yourself job goes well.

Saturday 21st: *Wonderful weekend for feeling in love. Success for many people.* If you've been apart, a reconciliation will be better than ever. There could be a small cut or burn.

Sunday 22nd: *Some guilt feelings. A quiet day, good for picking up the pieces.* You're asked to help but won't be able to oblige. You must persevere with your own routine tasks.

Monday 23rd: *A sober time, with a lot of catching up to do. Neglected tasks have mounted up.* You may get bored, and try to play truant. Your heart is really elsewhere.

Tuesday 24th: *People want to explain their feelings. Persuasive day.* This is an ideal time for you – lively and communicative. You may be speaking in public, perhaps.

Wednesday 25th: *Sweetness gets the better of anger. A kiss-and-make-up time.* A busy time. Pay attention to a personal relationship, or it will be starved of love.

Thursday 26th: *Lots of optimism. The softer, kinder side of life wins for once.* Someone may spring a lovely surprise on you, if you've been good in the past!

Friday 27th: *Still a gentle time. People should co-operate with each other.* A child who is normally a nuisance will be much more helpful. A neighbour may lend a helping hand, too.

Saturday 28th: *Smoothly flowing day. Lots will be packed into the time available.* Excellent time to concentrate on beauty – in the garden, perhaps, or fashion.

Wise Words for February

When you buy a pill and buy peace with it
you get conditioned to cheap solutions
instead of deep ones.

Max Lerner

March

Guide

There is an emphasis this month on your past, your own past, or the past of your family. You could get fascinated by your own childhood or genealogy.

In mid-month a somewhat sleepy mood overtakes you. Life is too much bother. You could feel rather depressed, for no good reason.

Then, around the 20th, you cheer up again. Your mood becomes ambitious, happy to stir people up. You enjoy meeting people, and may take risks with a friendship, just to see what happens.

It's a difficult month for getting entirely your own way. You may be frightened of rousing the anger or criticism of someone close to you.

WORK. Wages and salaries are on your mind. It may be time for the annual pay rise, or the Budget may well affect your take-home pay. The emphasis seems to be on a fair day's work for a fair day's pay, so don't expect any fancy increase without any productivity clause as well.

On the whole, though, I think you'll be pleased with progress at work. There continues to be a pleasant relationship between boss and workers, as though you're all aiming in the same direction – by no means always true in big business.

HOME. There will be talk about an elderly member of the family whose future will be causing some concern. But nothing will be – or need be – decided at this stage.

I don't think there's a danger of theft, but holiday arragements will be more complex than usual this year. You may think you've got everything organised – and then someone threatens to let you down at the last moment, and you have to start all over again.

There will be several comings and goings. Younger Geminians

may well be on the move. It's a good year for seeing more of Europe, ideally with some friends. If you live in the southern hemisphere, you may be coming north on a visit.

HEALTH. You could have a slight mishap from breathing toxic fumes. This could be a momentary alarm at your place of work, at a filling station, at home with a bonfire. No great harm will be caused: just annoyance.

It's a good time to give blood. If you are not yet a declared kidney donor, you could finally be persuaded to take the plunge.

Your own health could drop below-par in the middle of the month. It could be some kind of inflammation that lays you low. It will be made worse if you can't guard against it in time.

MONEY. This could be a financially lucky time. Gemini gamblers will enjoy a sustained run of good fortune, starting early in the month and continuing until the 8th or 9th. It returns at the end of March, from the 27th onwards.

There could be a small legal delay if you're waiting for a lump sum – a legacy, perhaps.

Expenses will continue to rise. Travel in particular will be expensive. If going on holiday, there may be sizeable extra surcharges to pay. A new car will prove expensive to run.

LEISURE. You'll take pleasure in reading and maybe writing, too. Lots of letters will go off, some to friends you haven't seen in ages. If you fancy yourself as an author, now's the time to set ballpoint to paper.

The garden should be coming along now, but you still aren't satisfied. Already your mind will be full of changes.

Plenty of socialising in the second half of April.

LOVE. Some Geminians are on the brink of a big decision in their love life. It is more likely to be an engagement than a divorce. Whatever you decide, you're happy about the future.

It's a much more successful time for well-established lovers than first dates. There will be a richness to love-making that depends more on familiarity than newness.

This is not a time for youth. Gemini women are likely to be drawn to older men. Certainly you will enjoy the company of grown-ups rather than the boyish type.

45

March

Key Dates

Sunday 1st: *A happy day. Some unpleasantness will be forgiven or forgotten.* There will be a surprise phone call. You'll feel more optimistic about the future.

Monday 2nd: *Good atmosphere at work. A time to get rid of a state of affairs that's outworn.* There could be a nice reunion, or a much better relationship with a colleague.

Tuesday 3rd: *A lucky day for many folk. Guesses and hunches are likely to be right.* You will be strongly impetuous. People will find you charming and humourous. Lucky number: 2.

Wednesday 4th: *Still lucky. Ideal time to feel love for someone close to you.* There's a terrific rapport with someone you live near. Ideal for travel and meeting new people.

Thursday 5th: *Slight quarrels at home. Mothers seem to get the worst of it.* Beware of feeling put-upon and hard-done-by, even though you feel people don't appreciate you.

Friday 6th: *Amid a broadly happy day there could be one slap in the face.* Someone will be much tougher than you expected. Officialdom may not do you a favour after all.

Saturday 7th: *Still a difficult time. Expect an explosion of rage.* Be careful with possessions. There could be a silly mistake in the shops. It's unlikely you'll have a quiet evening.

Sunday 8th: *Good weekend for travel, so long as you're prepared for surprises.* There could be a mechnical breakdown. On the bright side, you find something jolly to look at.

Monday 9th: *People are still inclined to fly off the handle at a moment's notice.* You are buzzing with Gemini ideas, but this isn't the ideal day to tell others.

Tuesday 10th: *Good day for tough-minded negotiations. There is a need for some escapist entertainment, too.* Try to get on top of your tasks early in the day. Take the evening off.

Wednesday 11th: *An ambitious time. Other people's feelings will tend to be ignored.* You're in a rat-tat-tat mood, wanting everybody to be efficient, punctual and helpful – or else!

Thursday 12th: *A cynical, worldly-wise time. Relationships are at a point of no return.* You'll be the one to make a break, if there's going to be one. Difficult links with Scorpio.

Friday 13th: *A spritely day, with one or two surprises. It's a loving time for most.* Perhaps it was all a storm in a teacup. Today you seem refreshed and tackling something new.

Saturday 14th: *A warm-hearted weekend, ideal for socialising and romance.* If you go to a party, you won't spend all your time with your regular partner! It's a frisky time.

Sunday 15th: *Some people will be stubborn and old-fashioned. Bloody-minded day.* It's best to keep out of the way. You're happier on your own, amusing yourself.

Monday 16th: *Still an air of obstinacy. A nice surprise in romance, though.* Someone may get in touch unexpectedly, or a bad mood will suddenly turn into sunshine and smiles.

Tuesday 17th: *An oddball day. People will appear arrogant and conceited.* Not an easy time if dealing with officials. You could have a bad time with a boss or customer.

Wednesday 18th: *A stable state of affairs will abruptly alter. Lots of warmth and aggression in romance.* If there's a sudden opening, you'll plunge in! A witty, self-confident day.

Thursday 19th: *Still a sexy time. Lots of desire and appeal for people.* You should be riding the crest of a wave at present. It's likely to be a busy phase in your social life.

Friday 20th: *Quite a relaxed, happy-go-lucky time, but with an underlying melancholy.* There may be a brief separation – or something that couldn't last has come to an end.

Saturday 21st: *Time to count cash and be thrifty. A stylish day.* You'll enjoy being out on the city streets. The countryside will seem dull and boring by comparison.

Sunday 22nd: *Good weekend for travel and adventure, ideal for sport.* Better for rambling etc. so long as you're in the right company. With dull people you'll go grey with boredom!

Monday 23rd: *A day of sunlight and shadows. Some good news, but problems as well.* Something goes wrong yet again. Perhaps it's time you replaced it. A friend seems rather catty.

Tuesday 24th: *Travel plans run into difficulties. People are not easy-going.* You may get a blank 'no' where at least you expected 'maybe'. Neighbours are up to something.

Wednesday 25th: *Much better. There'll be a good rapport and communication between people.* Sensible talking will iron out the problem better than throwing a tantrum!

Thursday 26th: *A wonderful day. Make the most of any opportunity coming your way.* Terrific if you're out on the open road. You'll enjoy impressing people with your knowledge and style!

Friday 27th: *The middle of a really lucky phase. The tide should flow in your favour.* Expect lucky breaks. One thing will lead to another. Ask favours, and you'll get the help you want.

Saturday 28th: *Another super day. You'll feel enthusiastic, hopeful and good-humoured.* You'll be extravagant and generous. It's a lovely time to give presents and treats to children.

Sunday 29th: *Doubts abound, but you'll still trust to luck. An untrustworthy day.* Perhaps you've said something in an unguarded moment that's come back to haunt you.

Monday 30th: *Some people will be scheming, going behind other people's backs.* To some extent you'll enjoy this, if you're taking part in a group activity. Office politics, for instance.

Tuesday 31st: *Time to put the past behind you. Don't let a nasty feeling obsess you.* If things turn troublesome, you're first off the sinking ship!

Wise Words for March

It is no good speaking in soft, gentle tones
if everyone else is shouting.

J.B. Priestley

April

Guide

This looks an amiable time. Although I wouldn't say you will relax – Geminians rarely do that – you will be in a pleasant frame of mind, wanting to meet people halfway.

There are nonetheless some problems to confront. You must watch out for a theft or other loss which could take the fun out of life for a while.

It's a good time to travel yourself, or to encourage others to do so. You will get actively angry with people who are very parochial in outlook. You're all for the wide open spaces.

You will be kept waiting by others, such as a local authority or other organisation, for an important decision. The more you harry them, the slower they'll be!

WORK. You will probably share an ambitious drive with others: either your own family will be behind you, or you may soon be joining a new team where there's plenty of enthusiasm.

You will try to get out of unpleasant duties early in the month. If you can send someone else, you will. If you can fob someone else off with a dirty job, you will!

There is news of an improvement in working conditions, perhaps not directly to do with your workplace as such. Possibly the district in which you work will soon have some exciting new facilities you can use in your midday break.

HOME. You could get involved with someone else's family this month. It's a good time to have a holiday together, or there may be some young marrieds in your neighbourhood whose company you're enjoying.

The second week brings the possibility of changes at home, perhaps because more room is needed with an extra mouth to feed for a while. With children going off to school you may want a complete tidy-up – to make the place fit for adults again!

There could be a burglar – or, more probably, child vandals, in your neighbourhood.

HEALTH. A pretty good month. If the pollen count is high this spring you could be suffering now and then from hay-fever, even if you took injections a couple of months ago.

If your own health is broadly okay, you could be worried about someone else's. This could be an elderly relative whose faculties seem to be growing dim, or perhaps a pet animal who is developing worrying symptoms.

Towards the end of the month you may fall into bad eating habits: too much junk food, irregularly eaten. Your digestion will soon tell you to eat some proper food.

MONEY. You will spend time with some well-off people. Don't try to keep up with their spending habits.

Unfortunately you are in an extravagant mood this April, and will overspend until you simply have to stop. If you have an overdraft, your bank manager will have some stern words.

If you're waiting for money, it's a stop-go kind of month. A delay early on will pave the way for a sudden payment later on.

LEISURE. There will be one or two big evenings out in the first half of the month. These will be expensive, which is fine if you enjoy yourself. I have a hunch, though, that you'll be dragged along – especially around Easter.

If you are giving people lifts, or helping to ferry other people's equipment around, check on the legal and insurance aspects. You don't want to end up the loser.

You could well be entertaining foreign children in your home, perhaps as part of a charity effort.

LOVE. If you are still in love with an older person, there will certainly be thoughts of marriage at this time. If there are problems, they are strongest around mid-April.

But you aren't depressed. Some Geminians will be getting intimate with a good, solid friend, and your delight in the love-making will be very strong. Perhaps you'll find that someone whom you always considered a traditional person is much livelier in bed than you imagined!

April

Key Dates

Wednesday 1st: *An ideal family time. People should feel close and affectionate.* You feel safe after a period of worry. Good day for buying something personal for yourself.

Thursday 2nd: *Still an excellent time to 'belong'. A great sense of family.* A nice day for a family outing. At work there may be a great team effort. Lucky colour: green.

Friday 3rd: *Lots of optimism, keeping fingers crossed, and hoping for the best.* You remain on a winning streak. Expect second favourites to do well today. Lucky number: 5.

Saturday 4th: *A lucky day for many, but high hopes could be dashed.* Don't put all your eggs in one basket. If you're in a perfectionist mood, you'll feel let down by one mistake.

Sunday 5th: *Hot-blooded time, with a good chance of success. Go for it!* Definitely the day to take courage in both hands, especially where romance is concerned. In sport you're a winner.

Monday 6th: *Very loving time, ideal for reconciliation or first love.* You may have thought you'd be nervous, but everything goes swimmingly. Good day for queue-jumping!

Tuesday 7th: *A day of drawbacks, travel delays, silence or bad news.* Perhaps you had built up your hopes too high. Someone with the initial G or P has a big impact on your life.

Wednesday 8th: *A restful day. Still the danger that you're being deceived.* As a Gemini, you're more likely to be doing the deceiving! Perhaps a lie has caught up on you.

Thursday 9th: *Hard-thinking time. A bright idea meets an obstinate obstacle.* You'll be slapped down for being unrealistic. Take extra care with figures, bills, accounts, etc.

Friday 10th: *Sexy and flamboyant day for many. Sudden passion erupts!* Perhaps there's been more beneath the surface than you realised. Good evening for making your feelings known.

Saturday 11th: *A weekend of steady endeavour. Not the time to rock the boat.* You may be taking part in a team effort. Good for concentration and stamina, but you'll be tired afterwards.

Sunday 12th: *A day when people with experience should be heard. Quite a lucky time.* You'll enjoy talking to older folk – for a while. Try to devote some time to a favourite quiet hobby.

Monday 13th: *A day of small mercies. Be grateful for them! Slightly sad mood.* You may be missing someone you like. Perhaps you'll be immersed in a boring phase of work.

Tuesday 14th: *The start of a marvellous phase for the family. Good luck and travel.* Your mood brightens, perhaps because of a last-minute lucky break.

Wednesday 15th: *Success could suddenly crown a complicated issue.* Travel problems that seemed insurmountable will now be solved. A busy, frantic day, with lots of energy.

Thursday 16th: *Not the day to step out of line, especially in romance.* Someone will be sharp-tempered with you. You'll be surprised how well you can manage without a so-called expert.

Friday 17th: *The start of a super holiday weekend, ideal for going somewhere different.* If you're in an exotic location, you'll be fascinated. At home you seem a bit cast down.

Saturday 18th: *An escapist day, perfect for getting away from daily routine.* Plan something different. You may be criticised but you'll be proved right – well, half-right – in the end.

Sunday 19th: *A wonderful mood within the family or another group.* Ideal time to be among a group of like-minded friends. You'll enjoy some friendly discussions.

Monday 20th: *Fantastic day for happy-go-lucky travel and trying something out-of-the-ordinary.* This Easter could be a truly magical experience, if you plan something special.

Tuesday 21st: *Still a lively, interesting time, with no big problems.* Good day to buy a raffle ticket, Premium Bond, etc. that may be lucky later on.

Wednesday 22nd: *Good co-operation, especially at work, sport or enterprising situations.* Be patient if waiting for money, but remind them that you are still waiting.

Thursday 23rd: *Lots of warmth and fellow-feeling. Ideal time to meet someone you fancy.* It may not get anywhere, but it's a pleasant contact. A day of small coincidences, too.

Friday 24th: *Friendly day, with no complications. Still a warm-hearted spirit.* Quite an air of good fellowship. One good turn deserves another. Help a neighbour to help himself.

Saturday 25th: *Nice steady day. You need to have a purpose in life to enjoy yourself.* If you're aimless, nothing gets done and you'll feel unwanted. Lucky number: 5.

Sunday 26th: *Some difficulties, but you have the ingenuity to overcome them.* You can pass on some tips to a beginner. You may be involved in research for a personal project of yours.

Monday 27th: *A practical day when solutions can be found to any problem.* Good for using your brain. Plan a little entertainment at home soon. You'll enjoy cooking today.

Tuesday 28th: *Striking day when there's an air of magic and excitement.* There may be a glamorous occasion to enjoy, even if you're not personally involved. Dress up to the nines!

Wednesday 29th: *Sweet-natured time when toughness gives way to sentimentality.* A difficult situation at work will turn out to be a misunderstanding. A horse linked with home will win.

Thursday 30th: *Toughness comes back with a bang! Could mark the end of something important.* Now the backlash! However it affects you, there's a feeling of being let down.

Wise Words for April

Professionals built the *Titanic* –
amateurs the ark.
                                        Anon

May

Guide

This is the month when you want to break free for a while. If you have been cooped up with business and domestic affairs for a long time, you'll want to take a holiday in totally different surroundings.

Whether you normally take a break at this time of year, I think you should in 1987. You'll enjoy a new experience much more than a visit to the same old place.

You're in a first-class mood most of the time. Although you want to relax, you don't want to let your mind get rusty. So you may be reading a good deal, perhaps painting or jotting ideas down on paper. You'll enjoy solitary pursuits like fishing, walking and sailing.

WORK. It's a straightforward time, except for two or three unusual occurences.

There could be a surprise about exams – not quite what you expected. You may do well in a subject you dislike.

It's a good time to meet with business contacts in unbusiness-like surroundings. You could get a free trip somewhere, thanks to a business firm.

You'll have been getting increasingly upset by one aspect of your working conditions. It could involve the toilets, catering arrangements or the hygienic habits of a few fellow-workers. Whatever the cause, you'll want things improved.

HOME. Your mind turns to genealogy for a while – that is, a study of family history. You may want to learn more about your ancestors. Alternatively, if you're still living in your home town, you may get upset with plans to spoil a treasured part of your childhood.

Teenagers who have found it tough to work hard in the past will now be getting down to some home studies. There will be more peace at home as a result.

If you are hoping to make changes to your home, with plans to renovate the outside or add an extension, there may be opposition from one or two neighbours. Perhaps there will be difficulty in getting permission.

HEALTH. If you have recently taken a holiday overseas, the home will be a nasty shock, and will swiftly lead to a cold.

If you suffer any chronic condition to do with the neck or throat, such as a goitre or frequent troubles with the larynx, I feel you would benefit from some kind of spiritual healing.

MONEY. Your savings could be boosted this month if you've had the foresight to invest in a foreign company. A sudden rise in share price signals the moment to take your profits.

If this happens in the first half of the month, you should invest your gains in some kind of high-yield government stock.

If you fancy a flutter on the horses, your lucky time seems to be around the 8th and 22nd, when lucky numbers could be 7 and 12. Broadly speaking, a horse linked with history could be lucky for you.

LEISURE. Geminians love the countryside, and you'll want to get away from city life as much as possible.

A touring trip round some of the beauty-spots of the country will cheer your spirit and make you fascinated about the varied past of the people who've lived here.

Neighbours will take a lot of interest in you. If you have tended to keep yourself to yourself, you will start to branch out, perhaps helped by a couple of parties in your street.

If you enjoy the seaside, beware of pollution spoiling your favourite beach.

LOVE. This looks perfectly enjoyable. I imagine you have just the right sweetheart (or two!) as there don't seem to be any important complaints. There seems, in fact, an air of abandonment – a desire to give in to pleasure and not be so stuck on the same old habits of love-making.

You will be somewhat more dominant than usual, wanting to be positive and joyous in your sex.

May

Key Dates

Friday 1st: *Slightly argumentative, but happy on the whole. Family squabbles, perhaps.* You may have to comfort someone who is going through a bad time. Boring but necessary.

Saturday 2nd: *You can't stay in a rut. Smooth running will be disrupted.* Children will take up a lot of time. If working for exams, this is a good weekend for getting on top of revision.

Sunday 3rd: *Edgy time for a while, but you'll enjoy getting right away from daily cares.* For some Gemini folk there will be a sweet surprise. Good for getting into the fresh air.

Monday 4th: *You'll hear a 'no' when you wanted 'yes'. A day of hard thinking.* Quite a tough time at work. There may be strings attached to an otherwise perfect scheme.

Tuesday 5th: *A super day, making up for the troubles of the last day or two.* You get an okay you wanted. Something may be cheaper than expected – or even free. Lucky number: 1.

Wednesday 6th: *Very lucky in one way, but there's also a drawback.* The two may be quite separate. The difficulty could involve a breakage, loss or carelessness.

Thursday 7th: *Happy day, but there's still bloody-mindedness in the background.* If there's someone in your life who enjoys giving you a hard time, you're at the receiving end again!

Friday 8th: *Ideal day to strike a deal, after a lot of argument.* Best in a work environment, but could also apply to any legal situation. Fight for what you want.

Saturday 9th: *Not a brilliant weekend. You'll have to settle for second-best.* The weather could spoil plans. Perhaps you won't be given quite what you want.

Sunday 10th: *More energetic, but there's a sense of doing your duty.* There could be a lot of strenuous effort. Perhaps there is also a subtle power struggle going on.

Monday 11th: *Something old and outworn will hold you back. Better for romance.* You should use public services as much as possible – cheaper and more convenient.

Tuesday 12th: *A sexy outlook on life. You'll be keen to see someone nice and attractive.* A happy, laughing time, all being well. Put one bad-tempered person out of your mind.

Wednesday 13th: *Thrifty time, so watch your pennies. Still a warm-hearted phase.* Perhaps you have been spending too rashly. Or there may be a bigger bill than you expected.

Thursday 14th: *Exciting, but beware of blowing a fuse. You could lose your temper.* Little children will be troublesome. You may worry that a friend doesn't like you any more.

Friday 15th: *Accident-prone time. Something smoothly running could go wrong.* You must be flexible in outlook. Go out of your way to impress someone with your good intentions.

Saturday 16th: *Still a potentially violent time. Don't expect a quiet time.* If a relationship is unstable, you'll swing back and forth between loving and hating!

Sunday 17th: *Still the possibility of disruption. People do not seem to want peaceful solutions.* Try not to attach blame to one person or another. See the situation for what it is.

Monday 18th: *High-powered time, with nothing going smoothly and steadily.* You may be busy or harrassed in several ways at once. A tiring day, but you have extra energy at present.

Tuesday 19th: *People want to take risks – without working out the risks involved!* You'll be one of them, and others may be trying to restrain you. Lucky number: 3.

Wednesday 20th: *A more sensible mood arrives. People with experience take charge.* You'll get some practical help. It's a day when the men take over from the women.

Thursday 21st: *A careful, painstaking day – but there may still be a surprise.* Good for facts and figures. You'll enjoy unscrambling a puzzle. You'll like people of your own age.

Friday 22nd: *Energetic end to the working week. Quite a lot will be achieved.* You'll have a pleasant glow of success. If you are looking for promotion, you'll have improved your chance.

Saturday 23rd: *A loving weekend. There's a lot of sensitivity in the air.* Pleasant weekend so long as you can concentrate on someone you love. Try to stop interruptions happening.

Sunday 24th: *An intense day, when one relationship really seems to matter.* A weekend for two would be ideal. There's a lot of telepathy between you.

Monday 25th: *You can't do exactly what you want. Rather a rebellious day.* Possibly you'll be prevented from tackling something you know you're capable of.

Tuesday 26th: *A more relaxed time. You have an appetite for something new and different.* A new movie, book, disco, etc. are all likely to appeal. You'll enjoy being quick-witted.

Wednesday 27th: *Someone tries something new. A surprising day.* There will probably be something new at work. It's a great time to be choosing a major new purchase.

Thursday 28th: *There could be a shift in family allegiances. Not an easy day.* Someone may give you a hard time, for no good reason. Relations between parents and children are awkward.

Friday 29th: *There's a feeling that something's gotta give! Slightly muddled time.* You'll be expected to bend to pressure, but you're more stubborn than they think.

Saturday 30th: *The muddle will lead to a firm decision. Quite good for the family.* Hopefully a solution will be hammered out. You are in a much better mood. Lucky colour: yellow.

Sunday 31st: *Still a nice weekend for family togetherness. Terrific for artistic activity.* Good rapport between the generations now. A family outing is a success.

Wise Words for May

Man must choose whether to be rich in things
or in the freedom to use them.

I.D. Illich

June

Guide

Most of June should be a relaxed and loving time. A big change which may have taken place in May has now subsided, and you're poised to enjoy yourself.

Early June could bring your pompous, snobby Gemini side to the forefront of your life! Try to relax and see other people's point of view. You may think you're superior to the people around you. Not necessarily so!

Again in mid-month there's the possibility of a quarrel erupting once more. This time circumstances will be against you.

The rest of June is broadly happy, though there could be one underlying worry.

Make the most of the sunshine – and your own sunny nature!

WORK. You could be on a refresher course, or will hear about a scheme you will undertake later in the year.

Some Geminians, looking for work at this time, are tempted to take any job, even though it's not suitable. You should hang on a bit longer. I feel the real work you're after will materialise in August.

Something you tackle at work may not be quite legal. It won't seem to matter at the time, but if the truth is discovered the work will have been wasted.

HOME. You will be pleased with the sporting efforts of children. There could be a small emergency where a child is surprisingly brave. He or she may become the leader of the gang, and be very popular at school or among friends.

There are no very clear signs about children, but I expect someone – if not yourself, then another member of the household – to be ill this month. The illness may not be bad, but it will linger, and slowly pass, I would guess, from one member of the family to the next!

HEALTH. Some Gemini people will be suffering from high blood pressure at this time – or, just possibly, blood poisoning caused by some mishap on holiday. Certainly your digestion is upset during June; but you'll recover fast, as you have a good constitution.

In the second half of the month, some Gemini people may have a slight mental block about going out and about too much. It's not agoraphobia as such, but you prefer pottering at home.

MONEY. You will have to pay your own way. Perhaps you were hoping that someone else would help, or even that you could get a grant or government subsidy. Well, no such luck at the moment.

Ordinary household expenses will be much as usual. You'll be very interested in how a friend spends money. There may be a few tips to pick up, and perhaps the share of a new possession between you – but this is less likely.

If you want to gamble, I recommend horses whose names are linked to members of your family. Any name to do with speed, light, fun or holidays could be lucky for you.

LEISURE. Most of your energy will be poured into your leisure hours this month.

Any connection with water sports, especially if you own or can borrow a boat, is very favoured at the moment. There may be a private swimming pool in your area which you'll be able to use.

It's up to you to entertain others. This may involve a party, house guests or visitors from abroad. If you're single, you'll find this interferes with your normal social life, and you'll have to cancel a few dates. But you don't mind.

You'll make an interesting journey this month, back into the past in some way. You could get hooked on an ancient monument or building, and want to delve deeply into its history.

LOVE. This is a good month for mental rapport. You aren't content with the physical side of love; you need real companionship at the moment. Without it, you feel there's nothing much in the relationship.

This is mainly true in the first two or three weeks. By the end of June you relax more, and don't put such heavy demands on the partnership.

June

Key Dates

Monday 1st: *A time when reality catches up with you. Perhaps there's a special duty to perform.* You may also be feeling ill. Don't spread gossip that could be unfounded.

Tuesday 2nd: *Quite hard-working, but it's not easy to concentrate.* You could well be feeling under the weather, without being sure why. There could be a small gift coming your way.

Wednesday 3rd: *Rows within the family, but it's better out than bottled up.* An expensive day. You can't stop spending cash, even though it's going on trivialities.

Thursday 4th: *You feel lucky, but it may all be a chimera. Don't count your chickens ...* If you get over-excited now, there is bound to be a let-down later. Still, it's fun imagining.

Friday 5th: *A day when many small things go wrong. Not a relaxed time.* You are up-tight and nervy, and the people around you will pick up the same influence. Not a happy day.

Saturday 6th: *A busy day, with conflicting attitudes around you.* You may be pushed hither and yon. You won't like a lot of crowds around you. Expect a headache or worse by evening.

Sunday 7th: *Oddball day. You'll want to get out of a rut, and do something different.* You're in a changeable mood. If there has been a worry over health, there could be an added factor.

Monday 8th: *A day of shifting moods. You won't be able to keep track of people.* Perhaps you're fussing over nothing. Try to adopt a tolerant attitude towards an arrogant person.

Tuesday 9th: *Problems suddenly abound. There could be a setback.* At work there's a confused situation, with lots of rumours flying about. You'll be worried about your finances ahead.

Wednesday 10th: *You'll continue to feel depressed – but mad as hell, too!* Remember that it could be an untrue rumour – or the situation can still be put right.

Thursday 11th: *Temper, temper! Everyone seems touchy today. Not an easy time.* You can fly off the handle easier than most. Count up to ten before saying something you might regret.

Friday 12th: *You want to break free from a boring, up-tight situation.* Friendly and affable, it's an ideal evening to try something different with a group of friends.

Saturday 13th: *Fast-moving weekend. You'll have plenty of energy and guts.* If you're on the road, you'll have a couple of near-misses or other excitements!

Sunday 14th: *A luckier mood. You'll be glad to put the bad times behind you.* If duty calls, you'll turn a deaf ear. You hear about someone else's good fortune or exciting plans.

Monday 15th: *Still jolly. There should be several moments of luck today.* Lucky colour is pink. Lucky horse could be one with the initial B or P. Healthwise the scene is encouraging.

Tuesday 16th: *Something could be snatched away at the last moment.* You'll be disappointed, but it may prove a blessing in disguise. You need some time on your own, though.

Wednesday 17th: *Changeable day. People will be unreliable and impetuous.* You keep changing your mind, because there are lots of possibilities. Lucky number: 3.

Thursday 18th: *One setback to your plans, but there's luck as well.* Someone at work will be competitive. Rather a moody day. You have the gift of the gab today.

Friday 19th: *Fairly pleasant, up-beat day, with some good news.* A small quarrel will clear the air. Keep up the pace, or things will get behind hand. A possession could be valuable.

Saturday 20th: *Nice weekend, but one member of the family could be fractious.* A child's illness could delay your plans. Good weekend if you have to study.

Sunday 21st: *Travel problems if you're on the roads. There could be a lucky break, though.* You could bump into an old pal, or discover something wonderful quite unexpectedly.

Monday 22nd: *If you're the inventive type, you could have a brilliant brainwave!* There is good financial news. Good time if you want to move savings from one investment to another.

Tuesday 23rd: *Hurry things along. Life is moving too slowly. Stubbornness in a romance.* It could be a clash of personality. You want to cope well, but it's difficult.

Wednesday 24th: *Some sadness around. People can't get through to each other.* A busy day. You may feel that a friendship is getting too much for you. Quite a good day for sport.

Thursday 25th: *A day of low spirits. Someone could do the dirty on you.* You'll feel let down, of course, and will have to start again – an awful waste of time and maybe money.

Friday 26th: *The tail-end of a difficult working week. Not a time to feel brilliantly happy.* This is the start of a better weekend than you expect. Plan something specific.

Saturday 27th: *You'll hear the sharp edge of someone's tongue. An excitable day.* You are brisk and sharp yourself, but should still manage to enjoy yourself.

Sunday 28th: *People – or belongings – get lost. An escapist weekend.* Maybe you are trying to tackle too much. Be careful near a hot stove. Don't leave fat unattended.

Monday 29th: *Still an uncertain time, great if you have no responsibilities.* An expert brings in a new opinion. You'll be busy on the phone seeing what the choices are.

Tuesday 30th: *Something finally gets finished. The end of an era?* Hopefully you'll be able to put something unpleasant out of mind. This could be a profitable day. Lucky number: 4.

Wise Words for June

Illness is not something a person *has*;
it's another way of *being*.
Jonathon Miller

63

July

Guide

This is a slightly mixed-up month, though nothing very worrying will occur. On the whole you should be happy, especially if you are taking a holiday somewhere new and exciting – with someone new and exciting.

There's a feeling of revenge early in the month. Why someone has wronged you I don't know. If you feel a friendship is bad news, it's better to have nothing further to do with it.

You could be feeling sorry for yourself in the second week, and fall a little ill. I don't think it will last long.

The third week is much more hopeful and positive, though you are still inclined to worry about the state of a relationship.

The end of July is a challenging time.

WORK. There are changes in the air at work. Thanks to the training you underwent earlier in the year, you will now be moved to a fresh position. If you're planning to change jobs altogether, this is the right moment to choose. School-leavers and college graduates will also find the right employment.

There could be a row over working practices – perhaps I ought to say *relaxing* practices – that have been in existence for years without anyone worrying. Now, perhaps with a new manager, there will be a tightening-up of discipline, and you may lose a cherished little bonus.

HOME. At some time in the first three weeks of July there could be a party at home. It could revolve around well-to-do neighbours: perhaps newly rich ones.

This could be upsetting to a child in some way. You may have to combine a party atmosphere with a child who's feeling poorly.

You can do someone in the family circle a good turn this

month, probably by putting them in touch with another married couple with whom they can become firm friends.

HEALTH. There could be further problems with your feet. If a corn is starting to develop, get it dealt with – and wear the right shoes from now on. The accent is really on preventive medicine. Take action now, and you won't suffer in the future.

If you are badly overweight, I feel it will be getting you down this July. Your whole psychic metabolism will get sluggish, and you simply won't be getting the best out of life. So make a special effort to slim – and stay slim. Once you've got the right willpower, it's comparatively simple!

MONEY. Your finances will slowly straighten themselves out. You won't be spending so much on personal items, though expenditure on children will be high.

If you eat out a lot, the bills will shock you. This is really the time to go on a crash diet; you'll be amazed how many pounds (of flesh) you can lose and how much money you can save.

Keep your bets open till the last minute. Changes in the betting will give you a good idea who will win.

LEISURE. You seem to be involved in charity work in a big way. Obviously, if this is a frequent leisure activity of yours, you'll be busier than ever, perhaps due to a special fund-raising effort.

Gardening will also be important.

You'll be annoyed that friends of friends are taking you too much for granted, wanting you to entertain them.

LOVE. There are two influences this month suggesting some more trouble to do with unfaithfulness.

Please understand that this will only apply completely to some Gemini people. It applies more to Gemini women than men, and if you are being unfaithful to your husband, you are most likely to be committing adultery with his best friend than with anyone else!

I can't tell which partner is more likely to be straying. It could be you, it could be your partner – and, of course, it could be neither. But even in the happiest of marriages, there will be some thoughts of love elsewhere, even if they aren't put into actual effect.

July

Key Dates

Wednesday 1st: *An explosive time in love. Expect a financial surprise, too.* Other people will not behave as you wish. There is a sense of disillusion. It could still end happily.

Thursday 2nd: *Pleasant day. People will be lucky out of the blue.* You can bring happiness where it isn't expected. Try to be as vital and lively as possible. Lucky colour: blue.

Friday 3rd: *Still a lucky time. Good for romance, partying and friendliness.* Plenty of fun in your life, but a figure of authority could stand in your way.

Saturday 4th: *Lovely, zippy day, ideal for moving around and travelling.* Other people put demands on you, but you can help them quickly and efficiently – and be on your way.

Sunday 5th: *Still a warm-hearted, sexy time. Not a terribly loyal day.* Expect some hostility within a marriage or affair if you act unfairly. You may be accused of being childish.

Monday 6th: *Make the most of your social opportunities. Good day to make friends.* You'll cope well, so long as you remain optimistic. Financially there's a small gain.

Tuesday 7th: *Slightly rougher. Good day for driving yourself hard.* Someone may have locked items away that you must get your hands on. A new store will have just what you want.

Wednesday 8th: *Some black moods, obstinacy and deliberate bloody-mindedness.* You're more likely to encounter them elsewhere than in yourself. Best stay out of the way.

Thursday 9th: *Things don't flow easily. Expect mechanical troubles.* If you work in industry, there could be management-labour disputes. At home there could be a leakage.

Friday 10th: *Luckier – and extravagant. Not the day to say 'no' to people.* You'll enjoy packing in plenty. If you burn the candle at both ends, you could fall ill.

Saturday 11th: *A day of deception and muddle. Someone could be deceiving you.* A day when you should have all your wits – but it looks as though you'll be forgetful and muddle-headed.

Sunday 12th: *A graceful, artistic and intelligent day. You'll feel good.* A brilliant recovery! – but there could be a relapse if you tackle too much. You're prone to a virus floating around.

Monday 13th: *A day to speak your mind. You have lots of persuasive power.* If there's a disappointing response, plan a second attack later. Don't give up hope.

Tuesday 14th: *You'll manage to get over a setback. Finances are a problem.* Frank talking will make life easier in the days ahead. A professional may act in a most unprofessional way.

Wednesday 15th: *A male relative is a great help. You can get plenty done.* You want to do your best, but it's hard to concentrate. You could make a silly forgetful blunder.

Thursday 16th: *A day of surprises. You can talk your way out of difficulties.* Pay a visit to friends, and plan something together for next month. Try to laugh your way out of a mood.

Friday 17th: *A smooth routine gets upset. Good links with the family.* There could be a happy reunion. There may be two clashing dates, so you look busy and flustered.

Saturday 18th: *A thrifty day. You won't be able to do what you want.* A trip may be called off. A political matter will annoy you. Someone close to you needs emotional reassurance.

Sunday 19th: *Edgy, restless day of arguments. Not a time to be shy.* Stay extrovert and jolly, if possible – and try to avoid criticising people who are doing their best.

Monday 20th: *If people are frustrated, they'll lash out. So don't expect good behaviour.* A fractious day, but some good can come out of it. There could be a surprise at night.

Tuesday 21st: *A jolly, laughing day. It's an ideal time to feel free.* Wonderful time on holiday. At work there will be time off. At home there's a special treat.

Wednesday 22nd: *Very lucky, but you'll want to spend plenty. Good psychic powers.* You can feel close to someone you love. Great sexual gratification if you take the trouble.

Thursday 23rd: *A down-beat day. You won't feel like getting much done.* A lazy day. You may play truant from work. One of those days when you don't seem to get involved in life.

Friday 24th: *Still a difficult time. Ill-luck will pursue a number of folk.* You could miss out by not being on the ball yesterday. A relative's bright idea won't work.

Saturday 25th: *Sexy day when you're looking for something different.* If single and fancy-free, you could pick up someone new. This could be the start of a nice friendship.

Sunday 26th: *Better luck. Good time to plan a fascinating venture.* You're feeling more cheerful. A disappointment will have faded. Could still be some trouble with a brother or sister.

Monday 27th: *The start of a long sexy period! Still a lucky time for many.* You should feel good, and be able to bring out the best in others. Dress appealingly, and be happy!

Tuesday 28th: *Slight delays possible, but otherwise a lucky time – in love and money.* You are likely to be happiest in a young crowd – especially on holiday.

Wednesday 29th: *Wonderful links with other folk. People want to co-operate.* You'll be lucky if you stick to your first choice. Keep in touch. Get phone numbers, etc.

Thursday 30th: *Good day for working hard until the job is finished.* A romance must be put on the back burner while you do something serious and practical.

Friday 31st: *Could be the end of a chapter in life. You'll bid farewell to someone.* For some Gemini folk this will mark a change in working life.

Wise Words for July

There are no gains without pains.
Adlai Stevenson

August

Guide

Life turns tougher in August. It needn't be nasty, but there's a serious, striving attitude to life. You'll be full of determination, but that won't be enough to stop several disappointments coming your way.

The self-confidence which has kept you merry and bright for most of 1987 will turn a little sour. Instead, you'll turn self-critical, querying every move you make. You'll be hard-headed, and somewhat suspicious of others. Maybe you'll feel you're being got at. There's a faint air of paranoia running through this month.

The more ambitious you are, the tougher you'll find life. If you are basically easy-going, not much will hurt you.

WORK. There may be a period of unemployment; it won't last long.

Developments at work could arouse your indignation. Whereas you thought everything was going well, you may discover that things are not as happy as you imagined. Perhaps a boss has been living in cloud-cuckoo land.

You could rub shoulders with someone you used to work with, maybe a long time ago. He or she could now be in a completely new line of work, and has probably done very well.

HOME. Children could be getting something out of proportion. If they are waiting for the results of exams, they could get a bad case of nerves. Your job as a parent is to provide firm, loving support. Don't add to their anxieties.

Another potential problem could come if your children have started to mix with much better-off kids with much grander toys, equipment, etc.

Household expenses must be watched carefully. This is very true if you are entertaining people in your home.

Some repairs needing to be done soon will materialise. Don't put this off for any length of time.

HEALTH. Some Geminian women reaching a certain age will start grandiose plans about improving their looks. Maybe after you have met a friend, you will consider cosmetic surgery and other expensive beauty treatments.

A healthy figure comes from a bright, intelligent mind. No amount of surgical carvery can create a beautiful personality!

If there is any ill-health in the family circle, a friend will help with nursing. This could especially apply to an infant child. There is a danger of a bronchial complaint.

MONEY. You won't like spending money on others. Gemini girls will be keen for boyfriends to buy as many evening meals as possible!

Someone – presumably an older relative – who has planned to leave you cash or possessions as a legacy may soon decide to make an offering now rather than later. This could be for tax reasons, but who cares?

If you fancy gambling, I think you'll be lucky at cards and bingo, but less lucky with horses.

LEISURE. You could get the loan of someone's possession this month. It could be a car, the use of a cottage, or some facility that's meant to be non-transferable. Don't worry, you're unlikely to be caught.

If you organise fun for others, you'll have some headaches this summer. People simply won't be grateful for anything!

If you have family visitors, it's worth quizzing older members about their own childhoods. You could learn a thing or two.

All artistic hobbies from painting to acting are favoured this month. Rowdy competitive sports won't appeal so much. A hobby begun earlier in 1987 will start to show improvement.

LOVE. This is only a temporary phase, you'll be glad to hear, but you may be feeling somewhat anxious about your love life. If your lover is a good deal older than yourself, the insecurity will be that much higher.

There could be a temporary parting, but this doesn't mean the end of the relationship.

August

Key Dates

Saturday 1st: *Nice start to the month. You'll feel warm and sexy!* There's a sweet influence encouraging tenderness and love. A friendship outside marriage could create problems.

Sunday 2nd: *You will act wisely, out of the best of motives. A poetic day.* You'll spend time with a sensitive person, and may be glad you're not so neurotic!

Monday 3rd: *Wonderful family time, with marvellous links with someone you love.* Even if a problem arises, you'll find a way to solve it with a minimum of fuss. Lucky colour: red.

Tuesday 4th: *Still a great influence, as far as the family is concerned.* There could be something special to celebrate. You seem busy making plans with others.

Wednesday 5th: *Someone will keep you guessing. Lots of passion on the boil.* You may have been taking someone for granted – and now you are uncertain whether you're in favour, after all.

Thursday 6th: *You'll try a new way to get what you want. A day of high feelings.* Excellent for romance. Good links with most signs, especially Aquarius and Virgo.

Friday 7th: *A real sense of achievement for many people. Good for travel.* You could win a prize, or spend time in wonderful scenery. Be generous with old possessions.

Saturday 8th: *A steady, comfortable day when the elderly are honoured.* You'll enjoy the company of an older person – maybe something of a father-figure.

Sunday 9th: *Nice family atmosphere – and good rapport on the sports field.* You'll be working smoothly as a team. It'll be nice to see youngsters growing up fast.

Monday 10th: *A slippery time when it's tempting to tell a lie.* You're on the fiddle in some way, or trying to queue-jump. You may end up worse than you started.

Tuesday 11th: *Back to normal. A day when lovers may reach a serious decision.* If you've had a wonderful love affair, you may part – or decide it's too important for that.

Wednesday 12th: *Quite a daring time. Something dangerous will be successfully accomplished.* At worst it could be a trip to the dentist. At best, a new skill under your belt.

Thursday 13th: *Still a courageous time. Something tricky will go well.* You feel fit and healthy, and may be playing a lot of sport. A new friendship is going nicely.

Friday 14th: *A day to rest and recuperate. Good news about exams.* Neighbours are friendly, and will do a good turn. Your strength of character may be tested.

Saturday 15th: *A day of serious thinking, with a hope soon to be realised.* You'll be looking at all the possibilities, but wanting others to help you make up your mind.

Sunday 16th: *A fun day, with plenty happening. You'll want to get away from reality.* Drink will go to your head! You need speed, good companions and something special to go to.

Monday 17th: *Still an enjoyable time, with a zip in the air. Very loving and friendly.* A child will do really well at a difficult task. There's one unhappy memory, though.

Tuesday 18th: *Another wonderful day, with lots of sweetness and grace.* Exciting times at work, with favourable changes likely. There may soon be a new project to tackle.

Wednesday 19th: *Everything goes well. A friendly, sociable time.* You should be floating on cloud nine. A mystery will deepen – then reveal itself.

Thursday 20th: *There's lots of co-operation and agreement between folk.* You must deal with a responsibility you have recently neglected. Financial arrangements need checking on.

Friday 21st: *Another loving day when everyone gets on well with each other.* A trip away from home will be spoilt if you leave something behind. Lucky number: 4.

Saturday 22nd: *Terrific weekend, with nothing hindering folk having a good time.* Be careful where you park, or you could be sorry. Expect a traffic jam, delay, etc.

Sunday 23rd: *A truly lucky day. You should feel you're riding the crest of a wave.* Ideal for seaside activities, or simply sitting out in the sunshine. You love the company you're in.

Monday 24th: *Bags of energy and enjoyment. You should have a stroke of good fortune.* Lucky horse could have a name linked with holidays. You'll be growing fonder of someone.

Tuesday 25th: *Very sexy and life-enhancing time still. Great for developing a friendship.* For some Gemini folk this will mark the time when you really fall in love.

Wednesday 26th: *Romantic, life-loving and still lucky – so make the most of it!* A happy time for all Geminians. Even if there is any sad news, you'll soon cheer up.

Thursday 27th: *Very energetic and self-confident, with plenty of luck still operating.* A sentimental day when you want lots of cuddling. You're getting closer to a couple you know.

Friday 28th: *A kindly and well-intentioned time. No one is trying to trick anyone.* There'll be a reminder of happy times in the past. Lucky number: 7.

Saturday 29th: *Still a warm, pleasant and loving time bringing people together.* Beware of an accidental cut to hand or foot. It could prove a nuisance in days to come.

Sunday 30th: *You may have to travel in difficult circumstances. An escapist weekend.* A special trip will be fun, but tiring. Beware of planning too much, and getting fed up in the end.

Monday 31st: *A happy, creative time, terrific for enjoying yourself.* Noise and excitement may be too much for you. I think you'll prefer a quieter day among lovely countryside.

Wise Words for August

Happiness makes up in height what it lacks in length.

Robert Frost

September

Guide

Whatever argument may have developed at the end of last month will continue into September. It looks as though your famous Geminian high spirits are a bit too much! Whether you are bargaining for a better price, refusing to budge from a negotiating position or sticking by your principles may all depend on the precise circumstances. But you aren't surrendering!

If you are in an emotional predicament, I can imagine you having fun, being sorry about it afterwards, but still being victim of your own strong feelings.

So it's not really an unhappy time, and I still feel it will work out well in the end. You remain full of hope – but aren't going to have the wool pulled over your eyes.

WORK. You may have knowledge of misdeeds by a fellow-worker that should be reported to a superior. Maybe it's to do with theft or another job.

If you have had a period of unemployment, this is the time when I would expect you to land a super new job. Geminians will be looking further afield than usual. Other ties permitting, you could well move to another part of the country – or even abroad – if the right offer is made.

HOME. This is a responsible time in family life. Some Gemini folk may be becoming parents; or the elderly relative about whom you've been worrying could become a real liability.

This problem seems to get sorted out in early September. What happens is for the best, even though there's some sadness involved. If you're expecting a child, there could be one moment of alarm either before or during delivery, but all works out well.

You're glad you've got the family near you. You could have one friend with no family, and you see how hurtful this can be.

A holiday with the whole family is quite likely, if only for a weekend.

HEALTH. You have a good constitution this month, and shouldn't fall ill – except for the first few days.

Your nerves, always the weak link in the Geminian constitution, will be a little frayed, perhaps because of someone else's vulnerability. But once that is cleared up, you'll be fine.

If you have a tendency towards depression, you won't be able to recover quite so quickly.

Beware of insect bites in hot weather. There could be animal fleas around, too, adding to your discomfiture.

MONEY. You start the new month in good heart, financially speaking. There could be several moments of good luck.

Personal taxes will be easier to cope with in the future. You may receive a special help, due to special circumstances.

In mid-month, however, you may find your partner has got into a financial muddle. You can help a married partner sort things out, provided he or she is completely honest with you. Don't just hand over money without being assured it will be spent wisely.

A further waste of cash could be due to your own careless or forgetful behaviour. By failing to pay a bill in time, you could be taken to court quite unnecessarily, and have to pay the costs.

If you enjoy gambling, you could be lucky with a bet on a horse whose name has some connection with yours.

LEISURE. You will enjoy meeting people from another country. You may find that, despite the differences, you have a great deal in common. If you live in a part of the world where two communities are daggers drawn there will be some effort to come closer together. Your courage and boldness at the moment helps.

Ideally this is the month when you should be thinking of next year's holidays, either getting some winter sun in Europe or, if south of the Equator, enjoying your long summer break.

LOVE. Clearly a mixed-up month for love. Although you have your differences within marriage, you won't find this relationship a great strain. If you have a love affair going, you may well want to spend a lot of time with your beloved – but I have the feeling that this won't be possible, due to other circumstances.

September

Key Dates

Tuesday 1st: *You'll be happy to bid farewell to a state of affairs.* You're still not as free as you'd like. Someone is still putting pressure on you.

Wednesday 2nd: *Still a pleasant, hard-working time with folk getting on well.* Better from your point of view. You may be busy trying to get your opinions known.

Thursday 3rd: *An inventive day. Someone may throw a friendly spanner in the works.* You make practical headway, though there is a setback late in the day. Lucky colour: gold.

Friday 4th: *A time to count the cost – but you're still in an extravagant mood.* A lump sum may be smaller than you think. A day when friends go their separate ways.

Saturday 5th: *Legal problems will finally start to be solved. There's luck in a serious matter.* Travel will be difficult to start with. A nice evening, even if nothing planned.

Sunday 6th: *A sober day thinking about the future. Something new will crop up.* You need time to yourself. You're not exactly moping, but you're not sparkling either.

Monday 7th: *Cheerful and happy. Things go with a swing, though you mustn't be silly.* It looks a busy day. Friends drop by, and arrange something for later in the week.

Tuesday 8th: *The same mixture – sunshine and scattered showers, luck but shrewdness as well.* You may be twisting someone round your little finger! Sounds painful – but ever such fun.

Wednesday 9th: *Hard-working time. Delays likely. Irritation in the family or another group.* A do-it-yourself job takes ages. An effort in the evening will only half come off.

Thursday 10th: *A bad-tempered day, niggly and ungenerous. A* *time to keep going – without joy*. A bad day for Gemini. You don't feel happy, and someone may shout at you.

Friday 11th: *Slippery and devious day. Someone does the dirty, and there's tension.* Approach a friend with a good idea, but don't be surprised if it's turned down.

Saturday 12th: *People won't want to be cooped up. A lively, adventurous weekend.* You're in the mood for fun, but you may have to leave someone behind.

Sunday 13th: *Quite cheerful. A day for getting plenty done as the seasons change.* Work now, play later. Get your head down and no day-dreaming on the job.

Monday 14th: *A warm and friendly day. Good for business, sales and committee work.* A bright idea has real possibilities. If you want to get ahead, make a move now.

Tuesday 15th: *A give-and-take day. There'll be tough talking, but agreement finally.* By saving in one direction you can spend more in another. Good time to give up smoking, say.

Wednesday 16th: *A change of pace. New proposals will appeal. Very modern and go-ahead.* Another opportunistic day for you. Think big, and have plenty of nerve.

Thursday 17th: *Still lively and forward-looking. The man in the house causes upsets.* Your boss could be troublesome, too. Don't let a row leave bad feelings.

Friday 18th: *Slight air of melancholy, also a snappy mood at times.* Doubts *won't* be quickly cleared up. You may brood about something that will never happen.

Saturday 19th: *Plenty of affection within the family. Any group wants to reach agreement.* A pleasant, fairly uneventful day. You'll be busy on the phone, keeping in touch.

Sunday 20th: *An angry day. People may lash out on the least pretext.* Muscles get tired if you work too hard in house or garden. Beware of machinery with a mind of its own!

Monday 21st: *A bit more cheerful and lucky. Not a loyal day, though.* You won't mind going behind someone's back, leafing through other people's papers – or even pinching something.

Tuesday 22nd: *Basically cheerful, but something unusual, even weird, could happen.* There could be a curious coincidence to do with events a couple of months ago – or even longer.

Wednesday 23rd: *Still spritely. A clever, observant day, with* *some incompatability*. You don't agree with a couple of people, but you'll still go your own sweet way – quite happily.

Thursday 24th: *A struggle for power – subtly, not with force. Family affairs important*. Warm links with a child who is going through a tough time. Some illness, perhaps.

Friday 25th: *Head and heart go different ways. Not an unhappy time*. You hear gossip that's not really true. You feel stand-offish in a romance, and won't be taken for granted.

Saturday 26th: *Fast-moving weekend, edgy and restless. Good-humoured time*. Luck comes in pairs. A favourite and fourth favourite could be a good double.

Sunday 27th: *Not a stable, steady time. Good day for thinking about the future*. You must help an older person. Quite lucky in the late afternoon.

Monday 28th: *Muddled day, nothing settled. Touch of violence in the air*. A busy, tiring day. Affairs are at odds and ends, with nothing quite settled.

Tuesday 29th: *Muddles get sorted out. People are more peaceful though there's still an explosive air*. You are more in charge of your own life. An expert may be annoyingly vague.

Wednesday 30th: *Quite a lucky day. People want to make a fresh beginning*. A happy home life, after a muddled few days. Good links with parents and children.

Wise Words for September

Grab a chance and you won't be sorry for a might have been.

Arthur Ransome

October

Guide

Quite a constructive month. You'll get where you want to go, but slowly and with one or two upheavals.

You aren't feeling very brave, all of a sudden. So you may lose some self-confidence, both at work and in personal relations. You value security above all. If someone threatens this, or raises question-marks about something you were taking for granted, your nerves will soon keep you awake at night!

Despite this mood, you're the one who feels you're holding the family together. Especially if you're a parent, you will exercise psychological power. You're the one that the others come to for advice and help.

Not an unhappy month, but a trying one at times.

WORK. If you travel in the course of your work, you may find yourself ending up in some unusual places this month. The weather will delay you – and a surprise is waiting there!

There could be a hold-up in communications. For some Geminians there could be a delay in hearing promotion results.

Work that was tackled earlier in the year will now have to be done again – this time properly. Goods that were ordered in the summer will finally turn up. This applies especially to computer installations, which will take months to get right!

HOME. There could be one absence from home this month. Possibly your partner is away on business, or has to visit relatives, and you'll be slightly at a loose end.

There could be an illness or uncharacteristic behaviour by one member of the family which causes mild anxiety.

If there's a toddler in the household, you will be pleased with his progress. Through him you may make friends with a new family in the area.

There may be a worry about a threatened rates rise, or a re-organisation of the rating system that will not suit you.

HEALTH. This should be a better month from the health point of view. You should be slimmer by now, and can slightly relax the diet you hopefully adopted a couple of months ago.

Keep up with the keep-fit work!

There are no other real problems this month. Your health looks good.

If there has been a dental operation waiting to be done for some time, this would be an appropriate time to get it over and done with. The same applies to cosmetic surgery.

MONEY. You fancy a fairly cheap October, and unless other members of the family object, that is what you'll get.

If there is an elderly member of the family who has not had much luck recently, you may be inclined, along with brothers and sisters, to spend a little more – to make life a little sweeter for this relative in 1987.

Gambling is not favoured this month. You are unlikely to be lucky in even the office raffle.

LEISURE. You'll get involved in collecting money – probably for charity. It's a good month for bring-and-buy sales, special sales evenings, jewellery or cosmetics parties and so forth. You'll enjoy yourself, and still make some worthwhile cash.

It's very much a month for shared pleasures. You'll be happiest spending your leisure hours in the company of like-minded friends.

If you want to take a holiday in October, the final week is the most appropriate time, especially for a touring trip in the car.

LOVE. A budding love affair may be running into difficulties. Maybe you met on holiday, and actually live some distance apart.

But an existing or long-term relationship looks terrific.

You seem thoroughly in love again. Emotionally this month is full of high spirits again. Perhaps you had a separation from this loved one, and are now together again.

Sexual compatability is important to Geminians. There is a good chance of achieving it now – perhaps better than before.

Good links with Taurus and Cancer.

October

Key Dates

Thursday 1st: *Warmth slips out of a relationship. Many people appear self-centred.* Illness could upset your plans. You'll be irritated with anyone trying to take advantage.

Friday 2nd: *Marginally uptight and bottled up. A nice chance for relaxation, too.* You may be off work. Someone may be off you. You're certainly off a person you're normally close to.

Saturday 3rd: *There's a return to the past, plus a desire for action.* Your mind could be floating back to a former sweetheart. You get on badly with Scorpio and Taurus at present.

Sunday 4th: *People are not inclined to give way. Hard-talking, fast-acting day.* You may go somewhere exciting, but not get terribly excited. A dream may be lucky in some way.

Monday 5th: *People act without thinking. Lots of confidence and style.* A good start to the working week. You'll turn on the charm. A straightforward day, without big problems.

Tuesday 6th: *There are worries about personal relationships. The truth comes tumbling out.* You have a new responsibility that brings hard work but lots of happiness.

Wednesday 7th: *Still a frank, no-holds-barred day. Good time to start new groups.* An outing will be fun, though someone gets alarmed. A row breaks out with someone your own age.

Thursday 8th: *People are prepared to take a risk. A day when the public is heard.* An exciting day, with lots of news. You'll enjoy getting on your high horse.

Friday 9th: *There's a new broom. People jockey for power. Good time to settle a deal.* You'll appreciate a lot of loving this evening. Certainly a friendly day at work, too.

Saturday 10th: *Peaceful, quiet weekend, except some men want to rock the boat.* Gemini women will feel pressured against their will.

Gemini men are more boastful and pushy than usual.

Sunday 11th: *There's a sexy mood, plus some shyness. Which will triumph?* You have lots of affection to give, and will be popular among the family. But a stranger will intimidate you.

Monday 12th: *A chopping-and-changing day. People are getting used to new conditions.* You get side-tracked by an unexpected turn of events. At home there's a cosy evening in store.

Tuesday 13th: *Still a mixed-up time. People blow hot and cold, not knowing what they really want.* Leave a fear at the back of your mind. Be lucky with an outsider beginning with F or M.

Wednesday 14th: *More optimistic. It's time to deal with an out-of-date organisation.* You enjoy the company of people who know what they want. Ditherers drive you up the wall.

Thursday 15th: *Happy day for most, but a nasty shock comes to some.* Keep up with repairs. Leave damage now, and you will be sorry later. You're in a competitive mood, and want to win.

Friday 16th: *The imagination gets wild and woolly. Good for creative work.* You're slow on the uptake, which is unusual for Gemini. Things old-fashioned will appeal to you.

Saturday 17th: *Lively and unconventional, but within sensible limits.* Gemini girls are looking for a man who can do things in real style. Time to plan something for Christmas.

Sunday 18th: *Free-wheeling sort of day. Happiness could burst out of nowhere.* Form-filling will drive you mad! If applying for permission, grant, etc, get all your facts right.

Monday 19th: *A moment of success in romance – or freedom from imprisonment.* There will be a consolation prize if you've just suffered a loss. Help a child who wants to be go-ahead.

Tuesday 20th: *The start of a broadly lucky, successful time in human affairs.* You pick up this mood fast. Your mood is cheerful, friendly and on the ball.

Wednesday 21st: *Very charming and sociable. People should feel in first-class spirits.* Ideal time for a party. You'll enjoy meeting new people. You won't be shy or nervous.

Thursday 22nd: *There may be a mild backlash from mean-minded folk.* Get immediate help if a machine lets you down. Delay will mean a long time without use of this gadget.

Friday 23rd: *Basically a lucky time. If in difficulties, there will be a lucky break.* Watch for a leakage, especially if you have sudden wet weather. Windows could give trouble.

Saturday 24th: *Hard-thinking day when extra brain-power is needed.* A pal gets up your nose with whining and moaning. Delays eat into your leisure time. Be lucky with numbers 4 and 7.

Sunday 25th: *Worry about an underlying state of affairs. This is a sobering day.* You'll do well in collaboration with other people, less happily on your own. Good for planning home changes.

Monday 26th: *Still a serious-minded time. Good time to attend to practical tasks.* You may be caught between two people, and not know which way to turn.

Tuesday 27th: *Deals are struck. A day of good fortune and new possibilities.* There's a lot of fun to be had – perhaps at someone else's expense. Links with another country are strong.

Wednesday 28th: *Versatile day. People will try something new, and like it.* You'll want to see a new movie or exhibition. An old friend may make a sexual move towards you!

Thursday 29th: *Well-meaning day. Some delays, but not serious ones.* You'll be glad the working week is drawing to a close. A day when you may feel under the weather, and need an early night.

Friday 30th: *Still happy and creative, with a spot of luck in love or money.* You seem to recover in time for a nice evening out. Waste time now and you'll be sorry later.

Saturday 31st: *A trusting-to-luck day. Things could turn out very nicely.* A half-guess and half-judgment will turn out right. You may well meet someone you've been longing to see.

Wise Words for October

The manner in which one endures what must be endured
is more important than the thing that must be endured.

Dean Acheson

November

Guide

Much the same outlook is apparent in November, too. You could be on the brink of an important decision, but your natural reserve and caution will hold you back.

It is wise not to lay down the law. Don't force other people against their natural inclinations. And, equally important, don't try emotional blackmail if you feel you aren't getting your own way. It won't work, and will diminish you in the other person's eyes.

Actually I think you will worry more than necessary. You'll be able to reach a happy compromise with most people in your life. It pays to keep your ears open. By being inquisitive you will learn plenty that will be useful later.

WORK. Not an easy time to make decisions, especially if you are a supervisor or manager. You will be frightened of what others will think. Actually, your freedom of choice is considerably limited, and if you wait a while longer you will see exactly what needs to be done.

There may be a half-offer from another firm or organisation. It will make you wonder what may come in the New Year. It's particularly important if a friend or neighbour is somehow involved.

Watch out for a thief at your workplace.

HOME. Quite an amiable month. Children do well, especially if they have just started at a new school or college. The friendship with another studious child seems to make all the difference, and the future looks bright.

A grown-up son or daughter who has been unhappy in love in recent months will appear more cheerful. You'll heave a small sigh of relief. Possibly your subtle nagging is now paying dividends. If a new sweetheart has turned up, you'll be glad.

HEALTH. The first couple of weeks could be wearing on your nerves, especially if there's been a career crisis. Although the signs are good for eventual success, the fight could have left you a bit exhausted.

Around the 12th there's some danger of a heavy fall, either by accident on a slippery surface or as a result of sport. You will have the breath knocked out of you, but no lasting damage.

If you are overweight, you may find this counts against you in a highly practical way. You may not get such good terms from an insurance company, for instance. This could be a wonderful spur to a slimming campaign, if you haven't started yet.

MONEY. Two extra costs are likely this month. You could be paying for some form of preventive medicine. If this is a joint effort with a friend, you will have to pay more than half – to start with, anyway.

Children again crop up. You could decide to make a special financial investment to safeguard their future in some way.

If you enjoy gambling, I suggest you pay particular attention to the Results column of the football pools.

LEISURE. It's a good month for mixing and entertaining. You will enjoy plenty of mixed company, and there is a special emphasis on married friends. Indeed, you could meet a new couple who fast become good friends.

You may be busy with redecorating at home. A casual interest in someone else's problems will lead you to investigate them further, and more fully. After reading up on the subject, you could become quite an expert.

LOVE. In the first week you will be fond and proud of your sweetheart, keen to encourage him or her in the world outside. You may have your doubts, but you keep them to yourself.

In mid-month you seem to feel sorry for yourself. You are looking for some loving consolation – and I see no reason why it shouldn't turn up.

The third week is homely. Again you'll get on well with a lover who can 'nurse' you, to some extent – make you feel safe and a little sentimental.

November

Key Dates

Sunday 1st: *People can talk themselves into – or out of – love. A sociable, conversational day.* Your sweetheart may be jealous. Perhaps you're making your feelings for someone else too plain.

Monday 2nd: *More changeable still – until something happens to leave no further doubts.* There's a hunt for a lost object. There could be trouble with a car – not necessarily your own.

Tuesday 3rd: *A point of no return, the ending of a chapter, or a fresh start.* Make an effort to keep up with the Joneses, whoever they may be! Especially true if you're entertaining.

Wednesday 4th: *Quite cheerful in the circumstances. Basically a loving, supportive day.* You seem a bit scatter-brained. It's hard to concentrate on the task in hand.

Thursday 5th: *Still lucky, looking on the bright side. Great for romance.* There's likely to be a reconciliation with someone who has been sulky recently. Lucky numbers: 6, 9.

Friday 6th: *Sexy and enjoyable, but things could turn nasty on the spur of the moment.* You could have more than one winner, so a double could come off. Don't push someone too hard.

Saturday 7th: *At a practical level, plenty can be achieved. In personal life, still warm-hearted.* Maybe you're daydreaming about someone you fancy. Lots of cuddles in the evening!

Sunday 8th: *Sexy and dreamy at one level, hard-working and successful at another.* You need a touch of glamour. You will enjoy a get-together organised by a local group.

Monday 9th: *People feel lucky and extravagant, but they're also slipshod and carefree.* Spend money on things that make you look marvellous. A practical joke will misfire.

Tuesday 10th: *Free-and-easy day, with lots of charm – and money being spent.* As soon as a quarrel breaks out, see the funny side. Friends from another part of the country get in touch.

Wednesday 11th: *Highly competitive time when men are likely to clash.* A piece of bad news will spoil a friend's happiness, and you must show sympathy.

Thursday 12th: *A tougher, hard-nosed time, with a strong whiff of success – for some.* A romantic tryst will be fun, but you may be manoeuvred in some way. You're not a free agent.

Friday 13th: *Still an energetic time. A clash of personalities is likely.* An idle remark could send shivers down your spine – but don't let it really worry you. Money is on your mind.

Saturday 14th: *A more amiable time when people want to relax in a spot of fantasy.* There may be a brief meeting with someone you like, but afterwards you go your separate ways.

Sunday 15th: *Easy-going day. Not many demands being placed on people.* There's a change in your normal weekend arrangements. You are busy sorting out Christmas plans.

Monday 16th: *Back to work with a vengeance. Not an easy day for many folk.* Your love life has a small complication, perhaps caused through working arrangements.

Tuesday 17th: *Success could be in sight, after a long, hard struggle.* There's some bad temper today, or a clash of personalities. Your strength of character sorts out a problem.

Wednesday 18th: *A time when middle-aged people do better than youngsters.* Good day for your love life, especially if there is quite a difference in ages. A coincidence puzzles you.

Thursday 19th: *An enterprising time. Experience counts. Good for business.* A sweetheart and you are thinking along completely different lines. You have to be courageous to get what you want.

Friday 20th: *Very lucky day for some people. A blessing comes out of the blue.* You should feel nice and attractive. If you are paid a compliment, accept it gracefully.

Saturday 21st: *Still lucky – also extravagant, easy-going, a great party mood.* You'll enjoy yourself with a small group of people. You won't be happy on your own.

Sunday 22nd: *Lovely family mood. Sensible plans will be made for the future.* Children are a joy, and show lots of promise for the future. Your partner is busy elsewhere.

Monday 23rd: *Still a close family togetherness. Good links within any group, indeed.* A last-minute alteration will throw your plans askew. Good help from a woman friend.

Tuesday 24th: *A sudden surprise in love. Good time to catch a stranger's eye.* You're in a very flirty mood. Don't snoop into someone's private life.

Wednesday 25th: *Still a lively time in love. People look for something spicy.* An enterprising day. The more you can help yourself, the better off you'll be.

Thursday 26th: *A day when romance matters a lot. Not the day for taking people for granted.* There could be a late delivery through the post. Not an easy day for Gemini housewives.

Friday 27th: *Zippy day, without any great problems. Several nice changes in the offing.* Be strong, don't waver. A romance at work will take a promising step forwards.

Saturday 28th: *Cheerful day when people exaggerate. Good for a party.* You'll enjoy the company of your nearest and dearest, but not for the whole day.

Sunday 29th: *Still a carefree time. People aren't in a fussy mood.* There's nowt so queer as folk – as you'll find out today. They'll say one thing and do another.

Monday 30th: *Amiable day. Things get forgotten or pushed to one side.* You don't care too much what people think. Aim to be efficient soon, if not today!

Wise Words for November

Life shrinks or expands in proportion to one's courage.

Anais Nin

December

Guide

After a fairly mixed-up year you should enjoy the closing stages of 1987. Several strands of your life will come together and make good sense at last. A mystery may be cleared up. And other people will be in the right mood to provide you with plenty of fun and entertainment.

Already your mind is turning to 1988. You will be thinking big, planning some important changes in your life.

You start the month in an efficient, no-nonsense mood, let up during the second week, let rip in the third week, and slow down to a pleasant, relatively undemanding final few days over the holidays.

December should be good to you.

WORK. If you help run a business, there will be renewed hope that 1988 will be a fine year. There will be promise of extra work, possibly linked to the United States or to a US company.

A fellow-worker will be reserved and cautious – too much so, in your opinion.

In you're a union member, there could be a new scheme in the offing which will affect your likelihood in the future. You aren't keen on the change, though you can see the possible advantages.

Your day-to-day working life seems busy right up to the break for Christmas. There'll be no slowing-off.

HOME. There seem no obvious family problems this Christmas. You may be spending more time with friends than the family itself. If you normally have a big family party, I doubt whether it will take place this year.

Individual family members are perfectly happy. One or more children could be taking a holiday away from the family.

Over the long Christmas break there could be some DIY work around the house. It's a good time for installing new electrical equipment, re-wiring part of the house, or taking delivery of new furniture.

HEALTH. If you have feet, prepare for them to hurt! They may get tired through too much standing, fighting your way through crowds, etc. There could be an accident (such as stiletto heel) or a bruised toe. If you have chronic trouble with feet, this is the moment for drastic action – perhaps even surgery.

Someone close to you could be suffering from a psychosomatic illness. Shrewdness is needed here, as a careless word could make matters worse.

MONEY. Ideally you'll have done some Christmas shopping much earlier in the year – quite a few months ago, in fact.

There could be a mix-up over one of your gifts to others. It could get lost, mislaid, or somehow be sent to the wrong person!

If there's an emergency budget you may find that your tax outlook is changed. Alternatively there may have been a change in company law in the past that you never realised. As a result, your tax situation will be less healthy if you run a small firm.

If you enjoy gambling, follow a steeplechase jockey who will have a run of luck just before Christmas.

LEISURE. It looks a helpful month. You'll be putting yourself out to see that others are comfortable and happy. This could be part of a charity effort, linked to voluntary work at a hospital or old people's home. Or a needy case could suddenly come to your attention, especially an elderly or poorly neighbour. You'll enjoy it.

You'll be booking for a holiday or education course taking place next Easter. You seem determined to get to a part of the world you've not ever (or properly) visited before.

Christmas itself looks pleasant if uneventful.

LOVE. Again the emphasis is on a steady, stable relationship at the expense of anything light-hearted. You will favour what is known and familiar. If you've been having an unstaisfactory love affair in the past few months, I wouldn't be surprised if you suddenly called a halt. Geminians do that, don't they?

December

Key Dates

Tuesday 1st: *Pleasant, warm-hearted day. People seem perky and friendly.* You may be looking after other people's children for a while. You come up against a fussy, faddy type.

Wednesday 2nd: *Slightly accident-prone day, but still a sexy time.* You may take a risk in love, especially if you're looking for a relationship outside marriage.

Thursday 3rd: *Good day for family affairs – almost telepathic rapport.* The work scene is boring. Avoid routine as much as possible. Someone is missing for a while.

Friday 4th: *Ideal day for appealing to people's better nature. But there's temper as well.* You feel nice and sexy, and will spread a little happiness today. Lucky number: 2.

Saturday 5th: *Could be trouble while travelling. Another day when everyone wants to spend.* There's a favourable response if you have a favour to ask. Lucky colour: gold.

Sunday 6th: *More travel delays and hold-ups. Minor irritations spoil the mood.* You are clever with words, and can win an argument today. Also a good day for mixing with well-to-do folk.

Monday 7th: *A bit more relaxed, but there are still problems to solve.* A pet animal could cause a mess or damage. Wear the right clothes for the occasion.

Tuesday 8th: *People find it tempting to tell lies. Facts are not taken into consideration.* You will be asked to join with others – perhaps to help the needy.

Wednesday 9th: *A rich, imaginative time, ideal for music and drama.* A better day for work prospects, with news of business coming to your area. Or you may be considering moving.

Thursday 10th: *Slight aggro over nothing. People are looking for arguments.* It's a fun day in your own heart, but the people around you are miserable. A special friend is clearly off you.

Friday 11th: *Vigorous day, with people going off at tangents. Poor concentration.* You'll get behind with daily tasks. One of those days when you're slow to make a start.

Saturday 12th: *Much better. A lot of luck and happiness for many people.* You'll enjoy the evening more than the day. Kids will cause some trouble, but in a lovable way.

Sunday 13th: *Still lucky. There's a glow of well-being round many people.* Domestic changes continue to preoccupy you. Good day to move things around. Lucky colour: grey or white.

Monday 14th: *More serious. People will work hard for a long time.* Move fast today. Excellent time if you're involved with education. You will be called to judge something.

Tuesday 15th: *A tough time, but also a serious time – perhaps the right moment for commitment.* People you want to see will be unavailable. Could be trouble with a cheque or credit card.

Wednesday 16th: *A day of low spirits and anxiety. But travel goes well.* You may feel sickly after an unwise meal. Christmas plans need to be adjusted in the light of a phone call.

Thursday 17th: *Still a serious-minded time. There could be some sadness.* You'll feel low. You may drop a brick, if you're not careful. You get on well with your own sex.

Friday 18th: *The bad mood lifts. This looks more spritely and interesting.* An evening out will be great fun, with the promise of more to come. Be lucky with friends.

Saturday 19th: *After the gloom of recent days, the desire to have a good time.* You will be welcomed warmly, if going anywhere new. But home is where the heart is.

Sunday 20th: *Quite an explosive time. Steady conditions could suddenly be upset.* A work problem in the New Year remains on your mind. You must rely on others for help.

Monday 21st: *Arguments and discord. There's a hue and cry over something important.* Health looks better. You may have been under-par for the last week. Someone tries to lead you astray.

Tuesday 22nd: *There will be domestic re-arrangements, just in time for Christmas.* A family problem is best openly discussed. There will be lots of last-minute shopping.

Wednesday 23rd: *An excitable day, full of chatter and good cheer.* The Christmas party season begins now. Everything goes well. Expect one or two gatecrashers.

Thursday 24th: *Friendly and smooth-flowing day, with no signs of difficulty.* A few last-minute arrangements, and possibly a scare over food or fuel. You're confused what people want.

Friday 25th: *Still a friendly day. Better to move around and mix.* You may see a parent or child in a new, pleasant light. Not a day to drink overmuch, or you'll spoil your evening.

Saturday 26th: *Pleasant and good-tempered. Quite a spiritual day for many.* Fresh air and exercise is what you need. Your mind turns yet again to New Year plans.

Sunday 27th: *Ideal get-away-from-it-all day, great for travel by air.* It is a day of high passions, with tempers flying at one stage. Let's hope there's some passionate loving, too.

Monday 28th: *Still a restless, travelling mood. But there is some deception, too.* Have a cleanout of room, cupboard, kitchen or car. You'll find a few forgotten treasures.

Tuesday 29th: *People will find it hard to think straight, but sexy and escapist.* There could be an unsettling link with an old boyfriend or girlfriend.

Wednesday 30th: *More energetic, but still an escapist, anti-realistic time.* Time to get away from usual haunts. A trip to another city will be exhausting but great fun.

Thursday 31st: *Pleasant ending to the year. Plenty of vigour and cheerfulness.* New Year's Eve goes well – but quieter than in recent years, perhaps.

Wise Words for December

Here is the Earth, don't spend it all at once.

Barty Phillips

Learning

More

Hopefully, in this book of 1987 predictions, I have managed to whet your appetite for astrology. Truly it is a fascinating subject, with far more depth and interest than you would guess from the usual Lucky Stars columns.

I have tried to translate the complex planetary patterns of the sky into straightforward, helpful words of advice. But, for all that, it's clear that a book applying to *everyone* born under Gemini – from the Duke of Edinburgh to Joan Collins – can't be completely personal. It can't deal with the individual problems and opportunities that confront you, and you alone.

That's where my Starlife astrology service is so useful. If you have any queries about this book itself – and if you want a more personal horoscope, based on your own date and place and even time of birth – do get in touch with me at the address given at the top of the order form opposite.

Regular readers will see that I've considerably expanded my range of services since last year. The **Birthday Horoscope** is still the standard report, if you want a detailed analysis of where your life is moving in the next twelve months.

But you might well be fascinated by **Who Were You?**, which looks at reincarnation through the eyes of astrology. Or there's the new **Biorhythms Diary**, ideal if you are training for sport, trying to lose weight, or simply interested in the daily ebb and flow of energy through you. If you have savings to invest, you will be intrigued by my specialist report **Stars & Shares**.

Whatever you want, apply direct to me, using the application form on the next two pages. If you live abroad, please pay by bank draft or international money order in £ sterling. Delivery will be about three weeks, and be assured that it will receive my personal attention.

ORDER FORM
Starlife, Cossington, Bridgwater, Somerset, UK TA7 8JR

Service	√	Price
Birthday Horoscope Your personal forecast for the next twelve months, answering your queries and dealing with any problems you have		UK **£8.00** Abroad **£10.00**
Who Were You? A detailed account, based on your horoscope, of the past lives you may have led, showing how – and why – you have today's personality		UK **£12.00** Abroad **£14.00**
Stars & Shares A personal investment guide, based on years of research, showing when, and with which firms, you can be successful on the UK stock market		UK **£20.00** Abroad **£23.00**
Your Biorhythm Diary A detailed daily forecast for the next twelve months, based on biorhythms and astrology, showing how fit, healthy and aware you'll be		UK **£10.00** Abroad **£12.00**
Personal Cassette An hour-long tape dealing with whatever you want – a child's horoscope, your own birth-chart – with complete individual attention		UK **£30.00** Abroad **£33.00**
Introduction to Astrology An audio-visual course for beginners, showing how and why astrology works. Six hour-long cassette tapes, with diagrams and notes		UK **£30.00** Abroad **£33.00**
Books on Astrology A book-list of further reading on astrology together with all Futura publications		**free**
Astrological Association Details of *the* astrological organisation **Faculty of Astrological Studies** Details of correspondence courses		**free** **free**

APPLICATION FOR HOROSCOPE

Surname	Mr Mrs Ms Miss

First Name

Address

Birth Details   Date [   ]   Month [   ]   Year [   ]

Birth-place

Birth-time (if known)

Personal details – absolutely confidential – ask any questions

Work

Home & Family

Health

Money

Romance